SELF-REVELATION THROUGH RELATIONSHIPS

PRENTICE-HALL, INC., ENGLEWOOD CLIFFS, NEW JERSEY

SELF-REVELATION THROUGH RELATIONSHIPS

RONALD B. LEVY

Department of Psychology
Citrus College
Azusa, California

Photographs for title page and chapters 1, 5, and 6 used by permission of Wide World Photos.

Library of Congress Catalog Number: 73–167896

10 9 8 7 6 5 4 3 2 1

ISBN: P–O–13–803569–5
C–O–13–803551–2

Printed in the United States of America

PRENTICE-HALL INTERNATIONAL, INC., London
PRENTICE-HALL OF AUSTRALIA PTY. LTD., Sydney
PRENTICE-HALL OF CANADA LTD., Toronto
PRENTICE-HALL OF INDIA PRIVATE LIMITED, New Delhi
PRENTICE-HALL OF JAPAN, INC., Tokyo

To Dolores

Whose loving encouragement and keen intellectual challenge have been with me in spirit and in body throughout the production of this manuscript. Through her my own self-revelation and my life have become far deeper, richer, and more meaningful than any printed words could ever say.

CONTENTS

PREFACE

The idea for this book came from a joint project in which the four of us who teach in the Behavioral Science Department at Citrus College were involved. We—Isaac Romero, Jack Spaun, Robert Schneider, and I—had decided to write a book embodying a new approach to the teaching of the beginning course in psychology, generally called Personal and Social Adjustment. The four of us met, discussed, and wrote over the period of almost a year. We finally decided that, due to many circumstances, we would not be able to produce the manuscript for this book. I am greatly indebted to my colleagues for the insights I gained as a result of our collaboration. While the present manuscript is entirely my responsibility, it did, in fact, spring from and profit by this experience.

I am further grateful to Isaac Romero who as my "amigo" and department head, supported me with his heart, as well as with his position, through all of the problems which I encountered in producing the manuscript.

The title for the book and the general theory involved in the ideas of self-revelation, I draw from the works of Sidney Jourard. His writings, particularly *Disclosing Man to Himself*, have given me much insight. I am also indebted to him for the many creative ideas he has given me at the meetings of the Association for Humanistic Psychology during the last three years.

I am indebted to Dial Press, to MacGibbon & Kee, and to Joan Baez for the privilege of using the material in Chapter 4 which appeared previously in Joan Baez's *Daybreak*. I gratefully acknowledge the permission of the copyright owners to use this material.

I must, of course, bow to my many hundreds of students at Citrus College—those anonymous ones who wrote the student-written materials in the text, those who enrolled in my classes during the past five years and inspired me with their ability to see and get to know their selves, and those, during the past year, who used the manuscript of this book in rough form. Without them this book could not be. May their sufferance of my experimentation help to make future classes at Citrus College more beneficial to those who enroll!

I am generally indebted to Citrus College, as an institution, and to my colleagues there, for their interest and tolerance with my, at times, somewhat unusual methods of operation. This kind of humanness and understanding is most necessary for one who wishes to do something new in the field of psychology.

I am particularly indebted to my colleague, William Schreiber, who read the manuscript in its entirety as well as part of the instructor's manual. It was encouraging to talk with him about his reactions to the manuscript and thereby to know better this economist with a heart.

I am especially indebted to my typist, Delinda Gloss, whose excellent work at the typewriter and keen ability to put my handwritten scrawl into readable form went far above and beyond what one might expect of any student assistant.

Finally I am indebted to Edward E. Lugenbeel, Psychology Editor at Prentice-Hall, whose gentle direction of this project has spurred me on many times when the going was very difficult.

RONALD LEVY

SELF-REVELATION THROUGH RELATIONSHIPS

FOUR STUDENTS IN SEARCH

1

Student 1

My name is Joe. I'm eighteen. I just graduated from Greenwood High School last June. I'm in college, but I don't really know why. Partly I don't know what else to do. My parents don't want me to hang around the house. I had a job in a gas station, but I didn't like it that much. People tell me that college is the way to success, more money, and all that, but I don't really like college. I don't like to study. I don't like to sit through those long classes. The other kids are ok, but I can't stay in the Student Union all day. Why am I here? I don't know. Where am I going? I don't know that either. I guess I'll probably be drafted and wind up in Viet Nam or somewhere else. I don't like that, but what can I do? Go to Canada? Not me, I like it here! Refuse induction? I don't like jail. So I guess I'll just go when my time comes.

I like sports. I played football and basketball in high school. But it's different here! Too much grind. Too serious. Besides, it takes up all your time after classes. I'd rather watch.

I do like the beach. I like to surf and in winter I go skiing. It's lots of fun. I have a buddy who usually goes along with me and we have a blast. Weekends we often go to rock concerts. I dig the Beatles—hope they're not broken up for good. I like Arlo Guthrie too, and Joni Mitchell. In fact, music is one of my main indoor hobbies.

Then there's my girlfriend. We graduated from high school together. I took her to the senior prom and we almost broke up. She didn't like it that I got a little stoned afterwards at the party. I guess she's right. Anyway we're back together again. She's here at college too.

Yeah, I live at home. Sometimes I wish I didn't. But my parents aren't that bad; they hassle me sometimes—when I come in too late, or when I don't seem to want to get ahead, but generally they're ok. My dad takes me on a lot of good trips. And Mom is a real good cook. It's mostly because of them that I'm in college. They have a real interest in me. Wish I knew what I wanted to do.

Student 2

My name is Sylvia. I'm twenty, almost twenty-one. I graduated from high school with a lot of effort. I got pregnant in my senior year, three years ago. Never seen the guy since—he split. I heard he's in the service, but I don't really know.

My baby was born just after my class graduated—cutest little boy you ever seen! Of course, I dropped out of school. They wouldn't let me walk around school like that.

No, I didn't work for awhile. My mom is real good. She took care of all eight of us kids, so she said she could take care of one more. 'Specially such a pretty baby! I stayed home for a while and then as soon as I could, I got me a job, waiting tables at a local hamburger stand. I didn't make too much, but it helped out.

No, my dad ain't around anymore. In fact I don't really remember him too well. All I remember is a big old man pushing my mom around and always being drunk. He left when I was five.

Sure, my mom works. She has a good job as a maid in a motel. Her hours aren't too bad and sometimes she gets extra tips, too. While she's away my older sister—the one who isn't married—looks after the baby. But my mom is the real boss at home. She tells Mary, my sister, just how to handle that little boy. She treats him just like he was her own—in a way he is.

Why am I in college? Well, I don't like slinging hamburgers that good. They told me if I got a little more education I might be a social worker. In fact it was the social worker lady who gives my aunt her check that told me that. I think I'd like that kind of a job—being with people right in their own homes.

Of course I want to get me a husband after a while. I don't like being home forever—even if my mom is good to us. And I certainly don't want to live alone. Why didn't I marry my boy's father? Just couldn't do it. Didn't love him. He was no good. And then he split before I could. But there's plenty of men around. No hurry: I want one who'll be a good father to my boy.

Student 3

My name is Randy. I'm just back from 'Nam. Put in my two years and now I'm out, thank God! Left high school in my senior year and enlisted. I knew I'd be drafted right after graduation. And then I wasn't doing so good in school either. Couldn't seem to concentrate. All I liked was sports and girls. My parents didn't really mind that much—guess they were glad to see me "safe" in the service before I got into any more trouble.

I don't like to talk about my war experiences. I have nightmares about them; that's enough. When you have seen your buddies blasted right beside you and you couldn't even find the remains, it's a real bummer! I never really believed I could make it—but here I am. If it wasn't for pot and other dope, I don't know how I would have made it. Calms you and makes you trip out from all the shit that's going on around you.

Since I'm back, I'm kind of restless. Can't stand living at home anymore. My parents are great, but they just don't understand. I have to have freedom—freedom from hassling, freedom to come and go when I want, freedom to be *me.* I see them once in a while—every week or so.

Yeah, I have a few buddies. Mostly they're guys who have been in the service, like me. Most of my high school buddies are halfway through college or married. I can't see the marriage bit and I'm not too sure about college—but here I am.

Why am I here? Well I got the GI Bill. And then maybe I can find out what I want to do. I have a part-time job in a garage, but that's not something I really groove on. I guess a guy ought to like what he earns his living at, but it beats me; my dad sure never did!

I live in a pad with a couple of my buddies. We enjoy life—especially on weekends. Shoot a little pool. Drink a little beer. Sometimes we get a little stoned. But I'm not too heavy on pot or dope since I got out.

What am I taking? Just what the counselor said. A few general courses: World History, Psych., Bonehead English, Intro. to Business. He said I might get some ideas about where I want to go in these courses. So far, I haven't, I'll wait and see.

It's sure good to be back. And a lot of the chicks on campus are real swingers. It's hard to keep your mind on business.

Student 4

My name is Janie. I'm twenty-two and I've done a lot since high school. Went to Coronado in El Paso, then to University of Colorado in Boulder. My father thought it was a good school—out of the heat, high, no subversive influences. So off I went.

Well I did ok the first semester. But then came winter and snow and skiing. I just loved it. And I loved the people who skied too. And then there was this guy I went with. He was a kind of SDS-type. We really had a ball. But he got busted for possession and I was kind of involved. So my parents thought a trip to Europe might help.

I hated to leave Boulder, but I did enjoy Europe. Particularly Italy—Naples, Rome, Florence. And I met this fellow there who showed me all the historical and artistic wonders of Italy. I guess it's because of Dave—that's his name—that I am still in college.

I went off with him and saw Athens, Israel, Cyprus, and lots of the Middle East. I really got interested in art, and culture, and philosophy and all.

Why did I come back? Well mainly money, I guess. It ran out and Dave didn't have any. And my parents thought I had cooled off—little did they know!—and ought to come home.

So here I am back in college. I really dig it. I love to read and study the subjects I like. And I'm doing pretty well, too. Guess I'll be a teacher of some kind. College eventually, but right now I guess I'll head for elementary school, not too young—maybe fifth grade.

What do I like to do? I love the outdoors. I like to go up into the mountains and just sit under the sky—day or night. Sometimes I take a book and sit under a big tree and read. And then I can listen to the other sounds—pine needles rustling, bird calls, sometimes animals.

I just love animals—all kinds. In my house I have a big Russian wolfhound. He's just like people. When Sergei rolls over on his back with his paws in the air and looks at me, he's just irresistible! Sometimes I think I love him more than *anybody!*

My major? Psych—yeah—psych. I want a degree in psych so bad my tongue's hanging out for it. I want to learn about people—most of all me. Sure, I love history and all. But I gotta know about people—how to get 'em together, how to love, how to grow. Some people think I'm a little screwy. Do you?

These are our "four students in search." What do they want? You will have to be the judge of that. Maybe it will help if we listen in on a conversation they had in the coffee shop of the Student Union. It started with Joe and Randy.

RANDY: Hi! Aren't you in my psych class—psych 45A?

JOE: Yeah, I believe so—in fact I remember now. You are the one back from Viet Nam. He got you to tell a little about yourself in class yesterday. What do you think of that class?

RANDY: It's ok so far. No hard assignments. Just a lot of bullshit so far. Everyone rapping on what they want. But I don't know where it's going.

JOE: I don't either. I kinda hoped it would help.

RANDY: Help what?

JOE: Well I'm not as sure as you seem to be . . . Sometimes my head is all messed up. I don't like the draft, but I don't know what to do about it. I don't like living at home but yet I don't want to split. I hate to get hassled, but I usually don't talk back. And I can't seem to make any close friends either.

RANDY: Well I have plenty of buddies. We go out and have a ball, but we aren't that close. My real pal didn't make it in 'Nam. Swell guy! 'Course I have the parent bit and the draft all behind me. But I see no way out of the job problem. I just don't seem to fit in today's Establishment. They've screwed it up so bad! How could anybody go for all that crap? Hey, here come two chicks from our class! Look at them! Wow! Hi! Come on over and have a seat! How about a coke, you two?

(Sylvia and Janie come over to the table)

RANDY: You girls are in our psych class, aren't you? Sit down! Sit down! Plenty room. Joe, get a chair for our friends.

SYLVIA: Well I can't stay long. Gotta go home and relieve my babysitter.

RANDY: Babysitter; You married?

SYLVIA: No—you can have a kid without getting married, you know.

RANDY: Yeah, I know only too well—almost.

JOE: But you're here in college. That takes a lot of guts. Is it worth it?

SYLVIA: I hope so. If it isn't, I won't be here long.

JOE: What do you think of our class?

SYLVIA: I just don't know yet. What I really want is a better job. But I don't see how this class will do it. I do like to get to know people though. I was stuck in that Silver Arches Cafe so long that I could smell onions in my sleep. I never had time to really know anybody there.

JANIE: Well I think our class is really groovy! I've been around a lot and I thought I had learned a lot. But suddenly I don't seem to know myself *at all!* I've been in so many messes and almost screwed up so bad!

SYLVIA: Well join the club, baby. Only mine wasn't an almost. But I think I know myself pretty good now! I learned the *hard* way.

JOE: What do you mean? You could make that mistake again, you know.

SYLVIA: No I won't! The next guy I get that close to is going to be my husband—and I haven't even seen him yet.

RANDY: Well I'll be damned! You mean no more sex till you get married? I always knew chicks were built different from guys!

JANIE: No we aren't! I mean not necessarily. We want and need the same things as you guys. At least I do. But I'm not about to make it with the first guy who comes around. I want one I can groove on *before*. Then maybe it's ok. But I get such conflicting ideas sometimes. They bother me! Maybe if I knew myself better . . .

RANDY: Well, honey, I would like to know you better and I'll trade with you. You tell me about you and I'll tell you about me. What are you doing for the next three hours?

JANIE: Not so fast, Marine. I'm no enemy rice paddy. But that's what I mean about that class. If we get in the act there we can all learn a lot more—about ourselves and other people too. Didn't any of you like any other people in the class?

SYLVIA: They're ok. But I don't understand you. Maybe if you had a baby to feed, you wouldn't be so freaked out on all this knowing people stuff.

JANIE: Maybe if you knew yourself and guys better you wouldn't have that baby!

SYLVIA: Well, you don't understand—and besides, I gotta go. See you in class, I guess.

RANDY: See what you did? Made her mad—and she's really sharp looking. I can easily see how she got that kid—*very easily!*

JANIE: Oh you sex fiend! That's all you ever see. It's easy to see what you did in the service!

JOE: Now take it easy, Janie, or he'll run off too. You may damage our Marine's tender feelings. Why do you always jump on people?

JANIE: I don't know. I wish I did—sorry, Randy. I really would like to get to know you.

RANDY: Ok, Janie, you're forgiven. You're too groovy to hold a grudge against. So we're all in this class. Do you really think there's anything there for us?

JOE: Well, I hope so. But I'm kinda like Sylvia. I don't see how.

JANIE: Well Joe, just stick in there. I believe there is. And I'm going to get involved up to my chin—at least!

JOE: You know, Janie, I'm not convinced. I may switch to sociology. How about you, Randy?

RANDY: Well for the present, it has the benefit that in that class I might be able to negotiate a liaison with certain people I couldn't meet otherwise, right Janie?

JANIE: Could be, Randy! I'll see you all in class. Got to run.

JOE: I *really* don't know! Randy, how did you ever get the guts to split from your family?

How do you react to these students now? Are they at all like any of your friends on campus? If not, how are they different? What are some of your friends like? At any rate, they are all *equals*—in other words, *peers.* And they do have various kinds of problems in their lives. Some of them want to know about themselves; others don't care. Some have trouble with adults—people in a higher status, authority figures. Some can't find their place in established society. But all of them want and need to get along with their own equals, their peers.

As you go through the chapters of this book, don't forget Joe, Sylvia, Randy, and Janie. And don't forget your peers either. There is much to be learned from them.

RELATIONSHIPS WITH PEERS

2

Who are your peers? They are individuals who are *like* you. They are neither above nor below you. They don't command you, but you don't command them, either. They are your *equals.*

But who decides that they are your equals? Who determines which individuals are your peers? You do. And no one can say a particular person is your peer unless you *feel* that he is. Being an equal—being a peer—is a matter of feeling, *not* a matter of measurement, because being a peer or not being one is not determined by *one* particular personal characteristic—such as how fast you can run, or your grade-point average, or the length of your hair, or the color of your skin.

It is true that a person may exclude someone from his peers because of one characteristic. For instance, I may not consider anyone my equal unless his skin is white, or unless his hair is at least shoulder length, or unless his ancestors came to this country on the *Mayflower;* however, making such a distinction does not mean that *all* white individuals or *all* people who have shoulder-length hair or *all* descendents of Mayflower passengers are my peers. If I make a point of any of these characteristics, I would also be unlikely to include among my peers those people who *associate* with blacks, "short-hairs," or more recent immigrants. In other words, although I may exclude someone for one characteristic, I include and accept a person because of my total perception of him. And so although I know specifically, by characteristic, those who are *not* my peers, I only know by my general perception–the *gestalt*—of a person, those who are my peers. Thus, it is often hard to explain rationally why a certain person is my peer, but the difficulty of explaining the reason why I feel he is my peer does not make me any less sure that he is.

So now you know what peers are. But where do you find your peers? At birth most of you had no peers—unless you were born as a twin or as part of some other multiple birth. You may have had older brothers and sisters, but when you were born, they were more like additional parents. In fact, you really did not develop as an individual person until many months after birth—probably at about eighteen months on the average. Hence you could hardly have been the peer of other children whose personal identities were already quite in evidence.

After you left infancy behind, however, you might have found yourself in a world where there were several others who received equal treatment from the "ruling class" your parents. If this were the case, these brothers and sisters could be your peers. You would accept each other as peers because of the equal treatment you received from above. However, if one or more of these other children—because of age, sex, or any other fact—received special treatment such as being put in charge of you, then they were not your peers. Of course if you were an only child, you would probably not find any peers in your family, unless your father (or mother) treated your mother (or father) so much like a child that you perceived that he or she received the *same kind of treatment* as you. In this case you and this parent might become peers—"children" under the same parent.

So it is in the family that you probably first found peers. But later on you went outside to play or explore your world. Here you found other people. Some of these people were like other parents. In fact, you probably called all men "Dada" and all women "Mama" until you learned that these names were reserved for two specific adults—your own parents. In this outside world you also found individuals who were not like parents—other children. Those at, or near, your age and size—who played with the same kind of toys, who wore the same kind of clothes, whose voices had a quality similar to yours, and who played the same kinds of games as you—would probably be accepted as your peers. You would not need to analyze all these factors; you would almost immediately know that they were your equals. And the acceptance would be mutual.

Later on you would go to school. Here again would be more people. But by now you would know that the teacher, the principal, the custodian, and the nurse were *not* your peers; neither were those very large children in the upper grades. However, in your class—and in other rooms nearby—were lots of other persons who clearly and immediately were your peers. Why? They received and accepted the same treatment from the adults that you did.

And so your experiences in life go on. In the military, it is clear that the sergeant, the captain, the major, and so on, are not your peers if you are a private, or even a private first class. Most of your barracks buddies are your peers. At work some of your fellow truck drivers, lathe operators, stenographers, file clerks, salesmen, school teachers, or reporters *are* your peers. The truck dispatcher, foreman, office manager, sales manager, principal, or managing editor is *not* your peer. The determination of who is your peer depends upon how you are treated in these situations and how you accept this treatment. For this reason some of your fellow workers will not be accepted by you as peers. They may not work as well as you, or they may work better than you. Hence they receive (or you may *think* they receive) different treatment from those in positions higher up. It is *your* perception of them in their relation to higher authority, reinforced by their perception of you and their reactions to you, which determines whether you and they see each other as peers or not. In many cases it may *appear* to you that whether an individual is your peer or not is *not* determined by you *at all*, but is determined by outside factors. It may seem that his being your peer is entirely beyond your control and is independent of your perception of things. However, it is wise not to accept either side of this question as a foregone conclusion or an unchallengeable fact. Check your perception out against your experiences. Think of a few of your peers. What is there about them which causes you to see them as peers? Has it anything to do with higher authority? Were they always your peers? If one of them used to be, in your opinion, a superior or an inferior and is now your peer, what events or changes might have caused this change in status or what changes occurred at the same time?

We must now make one point clear. When we speak of peers we are not just talking about friends—people you like. Of course many of your friends are your peers. Often, however, you may like a teacher, a coach, or a leader, artist, or dramatic star who is obviously not your peer. And on the other hand, many of your equals in school, in your neighborhood, or at work may not be people you like. Nevertheless, they have no higher or lower status with the authorities than you. Therefore, they are obviously your peers.

Now that we know what peers are and where we find them, let us consider *who* your peers are. Here you will have to give the answers. It will probably be easier to give these answers if you use the following questionnaire:

IDENTIFYING YOUR PEERS

Peer Questionnaire I

1. Think of ten of your peers—individuals who are your equals. (In making your selection, it may help to keep in mind the discussion of what a peer is on the previous pages).
2. Describe each of them in a short paragraph giving all of the important characteristics of each person.
3. Now answer these questions about them from your descriptions. If necessary, add to the descriptions in order to answer these questions more fully.
   a. How many of the ten are within a year of your age?
   b. How many are two years older? Two years younger? Five years older? Five years younger? Over five years older? Over five years younger?
   c. How many are the same sex as you are?
   d. How many are the opposite sex?
   e. How many have the same religion as you—either belong to the same religious organization or share similar beliefs?
   f. How many have different religious beliefs?
   g. How many are the same race as you?
   h. How many are of a different race?
   i. How many have about the same economic advantages as you?
   j. How many have economic advantages much different from yours?
   k. How many have the same political beliefs as you?
   l. How many have political beliefs different from yours?
   m. How many enjoy generally the same kinds of activities as you?
   n. How many generally enjoy doing things which are quite different from those you enjoy?
   o. How many were born in the same geographical area as you?

p. How many came from a different geographical area?
q. How many are about the same size and weight as you?
r. How many are different from you in size and weight?
s. How many have complexion and hair similar to yours?
t. How many have complexion and hair quite different from yours?
u. How many talk just about as much as you do in a conversation?
v. How many talk considerably more or less than you do?
w. How many make decisions about as easily or with as much difficulty as you?
x. How many make decisions much more (or less) easily than you do?

When you have completed this questionnaire, it may give you an idea of what your peers are like typically. You might then be able to answer this question.

My peers are typically of ________ age, ________ sex. They are of ______________ religion, ______________ race. They have ______________ economic advantages as compared to mine. They enjoy doing ____________, ____________, ____________. They come from ____________ (geographical area). They are typically ______________ size and weight as compared to me. Their general appearance is ________________. They usually talk ____________ than I."

If this paragraph does not seem to fit your typical peer, write another paragraph describing what one of your typical peers is like.

Now that you have surveyed your peers, it will be interesting to see how this data compares with the data which other students have collected about their peers. For this purpose you can arrange with your instructor to tabulate all the data and see what the similarities and differences are among the typical peers of all the members of your class. You may find that your peers are quite like those of other class members—or you may find that your peers are typically quite different from the peers of others. Whatever the result, there is no bonus for being similar to or different from the others. However, it may be a good idea to explore your feelings about the complete tabulated results. Therefore, your instructor may ask you to share these feelings with the others in a class discussion designed for this purpose.

GETTING A CLOSER LOOK AT YOUR PEERS

Now let us try another technique for learning about you and your peers. This will require you to answer four questions. In this case these questions must be answered more thoughtfully and carefully than the series of questions in the previous section.

Peer Questionnaire II

1. Select one of your peers—a friend—someone *close* to you. Imagine him or her as carefully and completely as possible. It may help to close your eyes and think of this person as *intently* as you can. Pay close attention to all of his or her characteristics which come to mind as you concentrate. Now write down a complete description of him or her.
2. Go over the description of your friend which you wrote in the first question above and underline those characteristics which *particularly* make him or her close to you. These would be the two or three of his or her characteristics which you *particularly* dig.
3. Now select another one of your peers. This time someone whom you know and have been with, but do *not* like and are *not* close to. Again close your eyes and imagine this person as fully and completely as possible. Now write down the complete description of this person.
4. Go over the description which you wrote above and underline those characteristics which particularly make him or her an undesirable companion. These would be those two or three characteristics which *particularly* turn you off.

Your instructor will probably want to collect these papers. He may also want you to do them anonymously so that they may be compared and discussed later on. For this reason it is also advisable *not* to mention the names of the peers you are describing.

The following are descriptions of peers given by students in a psychology class. Each student has described a positive peer and a negative peer as you did above. Those characteristics which particularly turned the writer on or off are italicized in the descriptions. Read these descriptions and answer the questions which follow them.

Student Answers to Peer Questionnaire II
(Questions 1 and 3 only)

Student 1

1. He is tall, has black short hair, fair skin, gives the appearance of being clean cut. Has a good build, but funny feet. Has a timid voice. When he moves he sometimes looks as though he is self-conscious, as though he feels there is someone watching him. He runs on his toes—really weird for a basketball player. He's very clean and neat except the hair on his head is receding. His eyes sparkle sometimes when he smiles. He has very small hands and feet. He looks best in heavy sweaters. He is always friendly, yet reserved. He rarely gets really angry, and when he does, holy hell breaks loose. He doesn't get that way unless he has good reason, though. He is gentle except when he's excited. He is usually kind to everyone though he is sometimes purposely inconsiderate to prove he's "his own boss." He is generous. His greatest fault is that he can be very irresponsible, or is reluctant to take some responsibilities. Sometimes he needs a little "push." He is very emotional, though he often tries to hide it. He sometimes resorts to "dramatics" in order to express himself. He is *extremely patient,* and will bend over backwards to *understand someone else's feelings.* He is very caring, and sometimes people take advantage of his giving nature. When they do, he gets very unhappy, like a little child, or perhaps very angry. But he is never in a bad mood for very long, never loses faith in people. He loves to clown around, loves to show his athletic abilities, loves to please others. *I like the way he touches me, his friendship, his love and his small sentimental gestures.*

3. She is short, blond, extremely wholesome looking, and very, very, pretty. She knows she is pretty and *uses others* to her own advantage through this. She has no regard whether or not she hurts them—is extremely selfish. She *has a phony manner* and *is selfish.*

Student 2

1. He is kind, *good hearted, generous*—he does not loose his temper, does not show his worry even when he is worried—*he says everything will be well to calm me down*—(because I am very wor-

ried at times). He is very helpful, friendly to others, and very *intelligent* and *observant.*

3. He is kind, good hearted, but not generous—he *loses his temper* for just anything—*he is rather stupid not very helpful.* I say stupid because he does not know how to talk with people and when he cannot convince you with his argument, he just loses his temper.

Student 3

1. I will describe a buddy of mine named Bill. He is a good natured Italian. He has a happy disposition and likes to joke. *He doesn't put people down,* but he laughs at some of the things people around him do. He is fun to be with and always ready to have a good time. *He listens when I want to rap about something and we oftentimes exchange ideas about work and school. I really dig the way he treats people.*

3. Joe is a person *who is "always right";* he is a person who knows more about you than you do; in fact, he *knows more about everything than you do.* He jumps around irrationally, makes weird gestures with his hands, and is quick to argue about anything you want to talk about.

Student 4

1. She is small and has some physical look I would like, but best of all she has the *most open mind* about things, everything. She always tries to put her self in the other person's place. She has the most beautiful understanding about children and patients that is unbelievable. She has been a very good friend to me. She has always been there when I have needed her. She likes me to call her to help me make some important decisions. We both have almost the same kind of home life. She has a way with people that's unbelievable; she is very smart, can talk with people about anything. But the biggest thing that has impressed me is her attitude and *understanding with children.* She is kind of hung up and is insecure in a way. I think this makes her so real. Because she has all of these good things about her. But she doesn't come across as a goodie goodie, and that she still has problems of her own. But able to cope with them not let them get out of hand when she talks to other people.

3. He is tall dark and very good looking. You are very impressed with his appearance. But when you come to know him. The biggest thing is his *phoneyness.* The way he *used people* to get what he wants and his bragging about how great he is with women. How he puts people down he thinks in a way where he comes across like he is joking. He has no respect for other people at all. Friend or not.

He will tell you about how bad he is just for you to tell him how great he is. He is just so phoney and he used people.

Student 5

1. The person who is really close to me is a guy whom I have known practically all my life. He's a little shorter in height than me and has a funny walk. He likes the same things I like and enjoys doing the same things as me. He is what a friend should be. Considerate, can be trusted, and is able to *handle responsibility.* He can take a joke better than most and isn't afraid to try something new. He has an *easy going attitude about life.* He is *a lot of fun* to be with because he is always saying something funny or got a new joke. Yet at the same time can get something done without a lot of messing around.

3. This person I also grew up with yet we went our separate ways a few years ago. We never really got along well because he was *more interested in helping himself* even at his friends expense. He has all the opposite characteristics of the person I've talked about in #1. He is about my height, blond hair, blue eyes. And smooth as ice with chicks. Yet he has made a complete shambles of his life. He has complete *disregard for responsibility* and consideration for others.

Student 6

1. She *cares about human life,* cares about Viet Nam, Drugs, and problems of society. *Enjoys life. Communicates* with me and listens to me. *Is open to criticism.* Is involved with student govt. Seeks to change for the better. Wants to help me succeed.

3. He *doesn't care about the feelings of others.* Lives now, doesn't care about what might be the results of his actions. *Takes advantage of people. Is only concerned over himself and over no one* else. To him life is wine, women, and pleasure.

Student 7

1. His shoulders are bent when discussing problem situations, or good and bad times. It gives him a look of humility. But when he decides to do something that he feels is right, his shoulders straighten and he has a determined look. I don't enjoy his ignorance on certain issues, but this never has overridden our friendship. I think I'm trying to say he is apathetic, which is not bad, if you understand why you are. He can obtain a childish look on his face during very tense moments, and in doing so relieves some of the tension.

He is open and level headed. I like his quest for Truth. Because of it we can relate without many inhibitions.

3. He is very messed-up person in the head. I once hated him, now I understand why he is and accept it. But I don't like to be around him. He cares very little about what happens to others as a result of an action of his. *His statements on life do not have much depth to me.* He constantly mocks those who stand up for what they believe if it differs with his beliefs. He is not open. He is easy to talk to as long as you are just bullshitting. When deep discussions arise he'll be responsive and be able to relate well until he tires of playing that game. *These discussions "seem" to be a game to him.*

Student 8

1. The person who comes to my mind is a fellow by the name of Jim Stevens. He is about my stature, a guy that has ambition. He is interested in girls and all the things that most guys are interested in. He and I enjoy being with one another and can talk to each other about problems and can share a different point of view. We like to hunt and we both have the same point of view. His outlook on sex is a little more liberal than mine and I think he tends to be a little selfish though he doesn't realize. *He has a friendly disposition, a very witty sense of humor. He doesn't worry about trivialities at least he doesn't let his fears dominate his personality.*

3. This person who I am thinking of doesn't have any ambition in life and *all he cares about are material things.*

1. *He has a sour disposition,* his attitude is that life is rotten.
2. He *indulges in self pity,* when he could do something about the things he doesn't like.
3. He uses his *church* and *religion* and *his defunct moral code* to cover up his insecurity.
4. He is *narrow-minded* and doesn't try to understand the other person.

Student 9

1. My closest friend has most of the same characteristics that I have. She agrees with me that morals are purely individualistic and what we do is our own business and we don't give advice to each other. We just tune in to one another and really communicate. She is really searching for love and someone to love her for what she is. A lot of people say she is fickle, but that is because they don't really know her. *She listens to me and doesn't put me down.*

3. This other girl has been a "friend" for 13 years. She doesn't really *ever communicate to me.* She puts me down for practically everything I do. She *isn't interested* in me, *only herself.* But I feel I

am the only one who knows and understands her and if I'm not around she would be terribly lonely. Our relationship is a one-way street but I don't mind.

Student 10

1. Ed is a strong person. He does his best whenever he wants to or feels it is important to himself. He has faults but that's what makes him human and close. (He's not an idol.) He seeks the truth and has faith in people (his friends). He accepts what he has (life) and seems to always progress especially when he fails. He's a good person (morals and virtues). He is really an individual (thinks for himself) and isn't afraid of anything in the world or in life. He's ready for the future and accepts fate. He's proud of his people (friends) and doesn't have to justify his actions cause in his self, he knows he's right. He really has class and a good soul. He *has the respect of others* by being himself. *He's human* (makes mistakes). He *appreciates life* and has love for close people. He has a *leadership ability* and doesn't have to be a phoney cause what he does is real to him.

3. Mary is a very dominate *immature girl.* She needs attention and will get it no matter what it costs. She *has to be a phoney* (not her real self) because of the guy she likes. She is smarter but brings herself to his level to communicate and understand. However, with all her faults, I can't dislike her that much because I understand her and hope she will "see the light." She's brainwashed herself to close off reality and strives for things she thinks she wants when what she really wants is true love. *She is a hypocrite.*

Now that you have read these descriptions, answer the following questions:

1. Are there any similarities in the characteristics mentioned in the description of the positive peers? What are they?
2. Are there any similarities in the descriptions of the negative peers? What are they?
3. Other than similarities (if there are any), what else do you particularly notice in these descriptions?
4. Is there anything worth mentioning about the *method* used in describing these peers—the kinds of words used, for example?
5. How do these descriptions compare with the ones you made in answering the questionnaire?
6. How do they compare with the descriptions made by the other students in your class?
7. Look back to Chapter 1 and reread the descriptions which the four students—Joe, Sylvia, Randy, and Janie—gave of

themselves. Which of their characteristics would you consider to be positive? Which would you consider to be negative?

8. Compare your answers with the rest of your class.

HOW DO PEOPLE RELATE TO THEIR PEERS?

In describing peers, people often mention the qualities of listening, helping, and communicating. Peers who have these qualities are usually considered to be positive. Those who lack them are usually considered to be negative. Let us, therefore, turn our attention to these qualities, and see if we can understand them more fully.

What is it which happens when successful listening, helping, and communicating are going on? We all know only too well what the absence of these qualities is like. Simon and Garfunkel have sung about it in "The Dangling Conversation," and Eugene Ionesco has written a play about it, *The Bald Soprano*. These outstanding examples of the lack of helpful communicating can be most illuminating in telling us what not to do if we would form a positive bond with a peer. We should not go off on our own separate "trips". We should not insulate ourselves from others with inanities which we really have no feelings about and which the other person cannot possibly feel anything about either. We should not talk *at* people—talking in their physical presence but only for our own benefit.

However accurate and valid these "should not's" may be, they are not an answer to the question. We need some kind of positive theory from which to operate. We need some statements about how human beings behave which may serve as a beginning basis for our efforts.

Here are a few such statements.

1. You cannot *really* help another person. All you can do is refrain from interfering with his helping himself, and perhaps prevent his escape from the problem which is facing him.
2. In view of the first point, it is fruitless for you to answer someone else's questions. Your answers will not be his. He needs his own answers, even if he begs for yours!
3. Your peer—if he is a friend—needs and wants your support. He needs your ear and your heart. He needs to know that you are listening and that you empathize.

4. He needs your acceptance—of his actions and of his feelings. He does not need to be evaluated or put down.
5. He needs a positive response, not a blank, cold mirror. Your expression of feelings about his situation may not solve his problem, but it will tell him you are there and that you have feelings too. It will also tell him you are getting his message—that you are listening.
6. He needs to be able to express his feeling fully about his problems. You might help by asking "How do you feel now about such-and-such?"

Now, of course, you may not agree with these statements. You may feel that when you help or communicate, it takes place in an entirely different way. But how about when someone helps *you*? What happens then? Think of the last good "rap" session you had. Think of the last good discussion you had with a friend about some problem of yours. How did this friend relate to *you*? How did he act? What did he do? Perhaps after you consider this carefully and discuss it with other members of your class, you can write your own revised theory of communicating and helping.

In any event, what follows in the next section is a series of situations in which students are trying to communicate and help each other. Read these selections and see which interactions seem to be accomplishing the kind of result you would want if you were in the situation. If they seem unfinished, suggest what might be done to make them more complete. If they seem to be missing the boat entirely, you might suggest how to redirect them—either in terms of the theory above, or in terms of your own experience. As a suggestion, you might want to role play several of these situations in your class and let the other students react to them and offer their ideas and feelings.

OBSERVING STUDENT INTERACTIONS

Situation A

SCENE: *Student Lounge (on a college campus)*

BILL: What's happening Joe? Haven't seen you around for a while.

JOE: I got busted. I was in for a couple of days. Now I'm out on bail. Trial comes up in a week.

BILL: What's the rap? Possession?

JOE: Yeah.

BILL: You're stupid to carry it around with you. Whenever I have any, I stash it outside in my back yard—or if I have it in my car I *really* hide it—like taped to the frame or in one of my hubcaps. You've got to be cool to outwit the narks these days.

JOE: But I don't have a car anymore. Transmission is all fouled up.

BILL: That's what happens to those automatics. I always stick to the stick shift. Wouldn't have anything else. Never know where you are unless your hands are doing the job. Those complicated gadgets are just money makers for the car industry.

JOE: Have you seen Tony today?

BILL: Tony? No, he and I don't hit it off too good. His head is all screwed up. He's really bad medicine. Well, I got to split, Joe. I got a date. See you around.

Situation B

SCENE: *Neighborhood beer and pool hall*

DENNIS: Hi, Ron! It's good to see you again! How long has it been? Must have been two years—that's how long my hitch was.

RON: Hi, Dennis! I heard you were back. It's good to see you again. Let me buy you a beer.

DENNIS: Ok, I could use one. It's really a hassle getting back into civilian life. I thought I was messed up over in Nam, with all that killing, and never knowing from day to day. But I'm not doing so good here either.

RON: What's happening? What bugs you?

DENNIS: Well I get back here from the Marines and what do I find? My girl's split. She went east with some dude and even her folks don't know where she is. What do I do now?

RON: These chicks are hard to figure. I'm wrong with mine more than I'm right.

DENNIS: Then there's this school bit. I split while I was in high school —remember?—never graduated. I didn't do too good, but I did get some kind of credits in the service. Don't know if I could cut college, going to class hour after hour listening to some creep tell me stuff I really don't care about. Why do they say they want a college degree for so many of these jobs?

RON: I don't know. Maybe it's just another way to put us down! At least you got your service out of the way.

DENNIS: Yeah! But this job thing really gets me. I need bread—unless I go back and live with my folks, and I couldn't hack that. Too much hassle. I'm living with a couple of guys in an apartment, but it really drains me. I had a little bread stashed away from the service, but I'm paying one third for this pad. And a part time in a gas station just won't do it. Besides, the job is really a bummer. Station manager is always on my back.

RON: Sounds like your head is really in bad shape. Well so's mine—and I got the draft board after me.

DENNIS: This place seems dead! There must be some action around somewhere. Let's split! Want to come?

Situation C

SCENE: *An apartment near a college campus. Kathy is sitting in the living room reading. The doorbell rings. She goes to the door.*

KATHY: Hi Sylvia! Come on in.

SYLVIA: Thank God you're here! I've got to talk to somebody!

KATHY: What gives? You look really upset!

SYLVIA: I've just split from my family. Things have been going really bad. It all began when I started going with Harry. You know him; he's in your psych class.

KATHY: Yes, I know him. Seems like a really groovy guy. Very sensitive eyes. Attractive long hair. What could be the matter?

SYLVIA: Everything! My parents don't like him. They don't like anything about him. They don't like his hair. "He's not one of us," they say. He doesn't have a job—or a career. Doesn't want to get in the war. Says he'll split to Canada first.

KATHY: That's really sad, Sylvia. How do you feel about him?

SYLVIA: Well, he's the only guy who ever treated me like I had more than a body. He is very gentle and loving. I really groove on being with him—every minute.

KATHY: What are you going to do?

SYLVIA: I've done it! I've split. I packed my things. They're out in the car. I have no where to go. I thought maybe . . .

KATHY: Yes, sure you can stay here—tonight. But what will you do after that?

SYLVIA: I don't know! I don't know what to do. I only know I won't go back to my parents. Not after tonight.

Situation D

SCENE: *In a drive-in movie. A couple are sitting in a car attending the show, but are not watching it. She is blonde, with an attractive face, expressive blue eyes, full lips. He is quite dark, with curly black hair, medium length. He is strong and determined in his appearance.*

RANDY: Patty, I guess I've gotten you into a terrible mess. I really took you on a bad trip. I never expected or intended . . .

PATTY: Randy, it's not just me who's in this mess—it's *us! We* have to work it out. I just can't do it by myself.

RANDY: Well, maybe I'm just no good for you. Maybe all I can ever do is mess you up. I really love you, but all I do is hurt you. At least that's the way it seems. Maybe I better just enlist and get away.

PATTY: What good would that do? That's just what people want. Or maybe that's what you want. I'd be left holding the bag, and it's getting harder to hold every day.

RANDY: Well, Patty, what do you want? What can I do? You know I don't have any money. I don't even have a good job. I have to keep my grades up so I can keep my scholarship. That means I can't work too many hours a week.

PATTY: Well, I can't tell you what to do. But I know for sure something has got to be done. We are getting nowhere. We talk around and around. I've sat through so many drive-in movies, I'm sick!

RANDY: I agree. This is what always happens. Each night when I pick you up, I hope something will work out, but after two weeks, *nothing!* We can't seem to help each other. We each want to work out some solution, find some answer. But we both block everything the other one suggests.

PATTY: Well maybe we need someone else to help us.

RANDY: God, no! I don't want anyone else to know. Enough people suspect already.

PATTY: How about John and Lenora? They were in a bad situation once. I'd trust them. At least Lenora.

RANDY: Well John is a pretty swell guy, but I don't know him too well. But I don't have anything else to suggest. Why don't you go and call up Lenora? There's a phone over there at the snack bar.

HOW DO PEERS RELATE IN GROUPS?

Up to this time, we have discussed peers on an individual basis. How do you react to a particular person? How do you work out problems between two persons? How can you help and communicate with another person?

There are other situations which many of us are faced with which are quite different from this one-to-one type of encounter. These are situations where groups of peers get together to do something together—not to simply "do their own thing". In these situations, decisions have to be made, plans have to be made, and the plans have to be carried out. Usually it is the deciding and planning which is harder to do than the carrying out. But snags and foul-ups can occur at any place along the road.

For this reason, let us make a few theoretical statements relevant to working effectively with a group of peers.

1. Although the individuals in a group are relatively intelligent and may have had very pleasant social contacts with each other in the past, they are nevertheless strangers as fellow group members. Their intelligence as individuals may not at all help them to get along with each other when they have something to produce together.
2. One of the pitfalls that new groups get into is to neglect each other and rush into the job to be done. However, no group can produce cooperatively if they do not know what kind of feelings, needs, and drives the others in the group have. Unless these are known, they cannot work *together!*
3. For this reason a new group needs to spend a *comfortable* amount of time exploring and getting to know the other group members before any attempt at the job—whatever it may be—can be productive.
4. After they have "broken the ice" and feel at home in their

group, the group needs to make some simple decisions about things which may seem relatively unimportant. For instance, they will need to be sure when and where they will meet to do their job. These simple decisions are simple only for an individual. For a group, these are as difficult—and as necessary—as a baby's first steps in learning to walk.

5. When a group is at least tentatively in operation, they need to survey the job to be done, to make a division of labor, and to assign some job to each group member. This will assure that everyone sees his importance to the group and therefore sees the group as important for him.

6. At regular intervals during their operation (the end of each meeting would not be too often), production should be stopped and each group member should be encouraged to say how he feels about the group's progress and about his part in it. The expression of any negative feelings and frustrations at this time should not only be tolerated, but should be strongly encouraged! This is like lubricating your car, throwing out your garbage, or ventilating your bathroom and kitchen.

7. If the group is to accomplish its purpose, someone must observe the progress that is made by the group and also the *processes* which go on in the group. This is like a person on an automobile trip keeping account of how many miles he has covered, which direction he is going, and how his motor is running.

8. Whoever is doing this observing will need to keep a *written* record of what he observes so that the group may be made aware of its progress towards its goal and also how its processes are working. If either of these phases of the group operation is neglected, the group will soon fall apart or grind to a halt.

9. Since most of us only know how to keep track of *progress,* the major emphasis in helping a new group to get started must be on the observation of *processes.* Learning the language of reporting and describing processes will help to sharpen the observation process itself. (For more details on this see the Appendix.)

10. If during the group operation, some group member feels the necessity to air his feelings, to call the group's attention to what is happening, or to ask a question, he should be encouraged to do so. This may seem like an interruption and a block to group *progress.* And it may be resented by some. However it is crucially necessary that this kind of interruption be done early in the group's life if the group's *processes* are to function smoothly. This kind of interruption is like

calling the driver's attention to his gas gauge, his oil pressure, or to an unusual noise in the motor. Unless he pays attention to these signs, the car may stop running!

11. After a major production has been completed—or at the end of the group's life together—there should be considerable time given to take care of any "unfinished business," to express any unresolved feelings, and also to say whatever each person wants to say about his experience in the group up to that time.

Now let us test these statements by seeing how they apply to the group situations in the following section.

OBSERVING GROUPS AT WORK

The two sets of reports which follow were written by groups of students in a psychology class who were planning a half hour record concert. The concert was to be produced in their classroom for their enjoyment as well as for the enjoyment of the rest of the class. The concert was to be representative of their whole group, so considerable thought had to be given both to the program and the production. They had just two in-class group meetings to prepare for the concert.

Group I

3/3

Joe, Evelyn, Mary, John, Sally, Norma, Henry.

Discussed odd things that we'd like to do. John dominates. Record concert. Folk-type music—*Greek* (Henry)

Evelyn from Monrovia.

Personal questions.

Henry wants to burn school down. R.C.

2001—Start.

All seem interested in each other.

Joe—Three Dog Night.

Thirties Music.

In the Mood.

I'm bored (Norma).

Joe suggests eating flag.

Shocked by Joe.

Joe interrogated.

John—Hollies.

He ain't Heavy.

Joe wants to play cards and is bored. Mary wants to go to Florida Easter.

Sally—Three Dog Night. Eli—*Something's Burning.*

Mood Set—for songs.

Few songs set mood with poetry—*Zorba.*

Simon and Garfunkel—Latest album, *Bridge Over Troubled Water.*

Keep Steady Mood—*2001.*

Poetry about Music to set mood—Greek (*Zorba*).

Poetry (Progression—Man feels how Pr.) Want to meet—Find someone who can get ahold of the sound track from "Wild Angels."

"Blues Theme." Seems that each group has the same type of people in it.

Group I seems very congenial—friendly
Group II indecisive
Group III Radical-type of group
Group IV Down on the world type—got along well

Personal thoughts—Norma. I felt that we got along well together. John dominated the group. However, it was in such a way that he tried to keep the ball rolling. Not many of us wanted to talk much. Comments now and then but not really a conversation. I felt that Henry didn't feel like he belonged; maybe it was just the new surroundings. Started talking about Record Concert with poetry intermingled. After awhile Joe seemed bored. Lack of communication. He thought we wanted long selections of poetry. Explained to him that the poetry would be short selections to set a mood—he seemed interested again. I noticed that Joe, John and I expressed opinions re. being bored. Although we expressed these feelings it didn't seem to hurt the relationship of the group. We were more open and at ease. Evelyn, Mary, and Sally seemed to listen and watch more than talk. They did contribute to the group as a whole but they did not try to dominate the conversation.

Evelyn speaking
March 5

At first we got off to a slow start. Two members were absent, John and Mary. John is the definite leader—with veto power. He has made most of the suggestions. The rest just agree and add their own ideas to his. He is really concerned that we do a good job. (John and Mary came in late.) As a group, we are pretty close, although we didn't spend much time getting to know each other by asking questions.

My impression is Joe doesn't like John giving the ideas.

John is getting frustrated with us. Either because some of us don't agree with him or we don't show enough enthusiasm with his suggestions. John feels this whole thing is one-sided; now he is calling for suggestions. We agree—he is frustrated. Joe is drawing Daffy

Duck on his desk. Silently he has become the center of attention and he liked it.

We are now getting all enthusiastic about leaving out the poetry and inserting different sounds for comedy instead of seriousness. It's something we all dig.

John suggests we "create a chopped record series concerning brotherhood—very satirical." We all love it.

Now our attention is scattered—maybe because we know what we are going to do. Mary feels sick. There are now many different conversations going. No organization. Henry complacently agrees—he's humorous. He gets embarassed and anxious when he is the center of attention. Sally is just enjoying the conversation. Norma is an active participant in all the discussions. John calls me "love"—I like it, but he seems to be a professional at it.

We are now giving our idea of "what is Peace to me" and we are thinking of including it in our record concert.

Group II

3/3

Before we really even got to know each other, we all decided that for our record concert we would each contribute a bit of music that we enjoyed so as the rest of the class can get to know us. We immediately decided on presenting our concert in the dark so that everyone will be more relaxed. The atmosphere seems to be important to each of us.

Next we approached the task of getting to know each other. It appears we are having trouble breaking the ice. We talked of several different subjects at first skipping from person to person in the group but it seemed we weren't really accomplishing much. We talked a lot and really didn't say much (of course only in my opinion). As time went on, and we got deeper in conversation, we became more open and revealed more of ourselves to the other people in the group. For awhile we all just talked, some listening to each other, and then we had our first disagreement. It didn't seem to sway the development of our group one way or the other, really. I think our father should be proud of us when we finally take our first steps.

Now we've returned to preparing our concert. It seems much easier in planning now. Perhaps we've started to crawl.

3/3—Evening
(Post-class
material)

After listening to other groups present their achievements, it was easier for us to see what is expected of us, and I think that we were, on the whole, satisfied with the results of our first day.

The members of my group felt that we sort of divided into partners for awhile. I felt we did, but for the majority of time and the most important part of our discussion, we responded as a whole. We all seemed involved and concerned in each other. For instance, when one person in our group was speaking, the rest of the group gave full attention to him and became involved in what he had to say. Then we would contribute our own views. All in all it seemed successful.

3/5

Today we discussed the record concert again. We'll have "2001," Joan Baez, John Mayall, Cream and Santana or Led Zeppelin. There was much cooperation—everyone tried to be as obliging as possible. Maybe that will change as we get to know each other better.

We'll all bring the lighting we want and set up an arrangement Tuesday.

Our difference of opinions is showing—GREAT! Now things are getting more interesting—it's about time. We enjoyed our concert very much. We had the total attention of the entire class, but it must be considered that we were the first group on, and everyone was turning to something new. ENOUGH. Don, Lou, and Sherm thought that the lights distracted the attention of the audience a few times. But Bill and Ben thought different. They believe that in order to have a good concert, the lights are a must.

Having read these reports, what differences do you find in them?

1. Do both groups approach their problem in the same way?
2. Is the participation pattern similar?
3. Who, if anyone, seems to take the initiative?
4. Are there any "silent partners"?
5. Which group you choose to be in? Why?
6. Are feelings expressed equally freely in both groups?
7. What is the pervading feeling tone?
8. What light do the six theory statements on pages 23–24 throw on the operation of these groups?

Many groups have difficulty being attentive to the nonverbal behavior of their group members as well as to the feelings which are present in the group. The following report is an illustration of one group observer who did catch the feelings, expressions, gestures, and other nonverbal messages of his group quite well.

Group III

4/23

Annette was puzzled at how to go about writing her feelings and observations. Her face showed her puzzledness. Shirley suggested silence and seemed to have a negative attitude at the time of her suggestion. She had a frown on her face when she suggested it. Cecile and Don seemed to be making the best of the time available to talk and they were enjoying themselves because they were constantly laughing, poking each other. Mona was laughing and seemed happy but she kept on biting her fingernails and had her hand close to her mouth at times. Annette was also nibbling on her fingernails.

Mimi was very quiet, and she hardly smiled. By 12:28 she had only spoke once—only to give a comment. Linda was going along with the rest of the group and she seemed happy because she was laughing a lot. Shirley after suggesting silence joined in with the group and also seemed relaxed and happy because she was also happy. I was also enjoying myself listening to the jokes being said. But I felt a little tense when I would look over at Mimi because she was too quiet compared to the others in the group.

The two sets of reports which now follow were written by groups who were planning a project to be produced for their psychology class. They had attempted this type of activity before so that they were more experienced than Group I and Group II whose reports you read previously.

Group IV

Sam
4/22

Sue, Laurie, Lisa, and me are the only people here from our group. The other 3 were not here due to unforseen matters. Everyone here seems interested in each other. I think we will have a good group.

Donna came over and wants to get into our gang.

Sue
4/24

One member, Lisa, is missing. Dr. Levy is giving us a topic to discuss in our group. Donna is even too embarassed to tell about her embarassing experience. No one else can think of any one event that was the most embarrassing. No one seems to want to discuss something that embarrassed them. They're talking about all different things. It's fun to watch people talk about being embarassed. (They're talking about it again.) Just talking about it and they get all upset again.

Five of us (Sam, Carrie, Doug, Ron and I) are very much at ease. Laurie and Dotty are at ease but don't talk as much. Perhaps it's because we 5 were in a group together before. Somehow we started talking about football and all the embarassing and violent things that happen.

Dotty hasn't said much so we all started looking at her to make her talk. She felt uneasy. It wasn't a very nice thing to do.

For a minute or two we broke up into little groups, talking. I don't like it when that happens. Dotty's talking a lot more now.

Ron's talking. Everyone's listening but Carrie seems very preoccupied.

Time for our topic is up.

Dotty
4/29

Sue thought of some topics—would've liked to do it on death but Carrie has an aversion to this topic so we're not doing it. Also maybe love and hate or fear or something along that line.

Donna picked our presentation date. We're first—this brought on mixed feelings of dread and relief at getting it over.

Everyone seems interested in what the group's talking about. No one seems to be left out or ill at ease.

Carrie suggested how dogs and their masters resemble one another.

We're discussing what Tim's group is doing—the All-American Boy.

Donna and Sam are constantly teasing and bickering amongst themselves—creates happiness in that area.

Lisa suggested humor.

Sam suggested values—general response is that it would be a difficult topic. Everyone's lost in thought again. Just sort of lazily sitting around.

Reincarnation as a topic is brought up.

Inborn fears brought up.

We all think it's so much harder to think of a topic this time—maybe because our presentation is supposed to be better and there's more pressure involving the time.

Topic—violence. This brought a negative reaction. Everyone's tired of violence—there's too much of it around us every day.

They're talking about their own dogs now.

Sue said something that makes me think she resents her mother somewhat.

We're still on our own pets. When talking of them, their voice acquires an affectionate intonation but most of the stories end sad because their pets have died.

Sue suggested making a movie—Linda has a camera and projector. This topic is emanating more interest. Perhaps we'll do it on this.

All Sam likes to do, it seems like, is drink wine. No matter what we're talking about he interjects something about drinking wine. I think he's only kidding—everyone accepts it as his standard joke.

Now we're thinking of different things to take pictures of for our movie relating to the topic of what makes people happy.

Discussing "A Black Girl in Seach of Her God"—this leads to the conversation on not having money.

Everyone got a good laugh at a situation where two people were talking about the same thing but thinking about two different things which led to a rather funny play on words.

Lisa
5/6

All gave reasons why didn't show up for meeting . . . Ron, Betty, and Laurie are not present . . . Sam had a bad hangover . . . Carrie is in an upset and disgusting mood. She really doesn't care now . . . Ron showed up late today . . .

We changed our method of presentation . . . Donna is very silent . . . but then tells us what's on her mind . . ., she is too upset about no one showing up . . .

Carrie seems to have taken over the group . . . the main talker . . . Sue tries to change her by agreeing . . .

We changed the subject to cars . . . the one he's had had personality . . . it clunks, says Sue . . .

Sue brought a friend, Sam . . . he is very quiet . . . he smiles occasionally . . . Sue seems to have a sneaking expression in her actions and eyes . . .

No one seems to keep to the subject . . . Everything from . . . the BSU to the coliseum to happiness . . .

Sam is very quiet in his voice today . . . Maybe . . . it's because he didn't show up . . .

Donna seems happy when she talks about children . . . their actions.

Sam (the new member) is asked his action on happiness . . . he smiles and then gets hit by Sue . . . not that Sam . . .

Donna is interested in dancing . . . the music . . . Carrie also . . . but they had a dance . . . Carrie's upset . . . the right to also . . . her wallet was stolen . . .

Carrie is self conscious . . . her nose . . . she scratched it . . .

Having money makes them all smile . . . but money is a bind . . . You can't enjoy the real life you have to live . . .

Carrie has now become reserved again . . . she was really burnt up about no one showing up . . .

Our problem now is time . . . Ron seems to agree with everything that Carrie says . . . even though he seems not to come through in the end . . .

A sudden interruption . . . Tim does his flip . . . for the day . . .

Our group is splitting up to . . . talk to others . . . Donna is not accepted in the other group . . . Once you leave . . . you can't come back . . .

The smoke is bothering Carrie and she gets up to leave.

Our discussion is over and the discussion leads to Sue's measles . . . Sue is the personality . . . of our group . . . she is our happiness sign . . . Carrie is our leader but . . . very quiet today . . . Donna . . . is not too interested . . . Sam is reserved for not showing up . . . Ron is quiet but doesn't feel any guilt of not showing up . . . and Sam (our new member) has been accepted by all . . .

I myself really enjoy this group it has that certain personality . . .

Laurie
5/12

In the first place, lack of attendance among our members is making it difficult. Sue has come to the point. Although we are considerably behind, no one is worried; we'll make it. Carrie seems more enthusiastic since last time and this boy Ron hasn't said much. Lisa just got here so we're gradually becoming a group again. She immediately begins telling us of her contribution to the group, and now everybody is talking. This meeting seems well-balanced and I think the participation is excellent. All of a sudden Donna is strangely silent. Ron seems determined on setting up an out-of-class meeting. Meanwhile Carrie and Sue are concerned with the organization of the presentation. Now Sue relates a few examples of happiness (of all things) which she has seen in the past week. Her stories seem to amuse and entertain the other members of the group. Everything is smooth except Donna is still strangely silent. Again talk goes back to organization for the presentation. Donna at long last makes a couple of suggestions and hopefully this is some sort of indication. We're now thinking of music for the presentation and everybody says something! Donna is now talking, but Ron is silent. We can't get everybody to talk at once. We've figured where the meeting will be held and everybody seems understandably relieved! While Sue draws a map to her house, Donna and Carrie carry on some sort of conversation none of which I can hear. Somehow the talk has shifted and Sue now tells us of her duties as a "housemaid" and cook, yet everybody seems interested. I forgot all about Lisa, because she's over my shoulder and now says nothing.

Carrie's plans for the presentation are good and are being accepted by everyone except Lisa, who is still quiet. Again the scene changes as everybody reminisces about their experiences at the all-night party at Disneyland in their senior year of high school. Now everybody seems to pay attention to Group 4 because of the noise and clatter they have caused. All of a sudden small, little conversations emerge throughout the group and Lisa is talking again. And better yet, everybody is talking! We've finally gotten together. It now seems just like a "bull-session" as everybody relates past, personal experiences of the week. Everybody is talkative, and smiling and laughing. Good sign! Nobody seems interested in the presentation now. Although this is our last day in class, we all feel confident of the outcome of our presentation. Time is up!

Group V

Vic
April 22

This is our first meeting. I like this group. There is a feeling of well being. The people seem relaxed. Tim is already talking about his ideas for a presentation. The people are already rapping about different things. Tim gives me the feeling of being a leader. He likes to do most of the talking.

Ruby is quite self-conscious. She seems defensive when someone talks to her.

I have a feeling this group will be more efficient than the last one I was in.

We are much freer than the first meeting of my last group. Everyone was more used to the group idea and could let go more easily.

Louise
April 24

Most embarassing thing and why?

We all are just sitting around staring and chomping gum.

Ruby started out telling one of her experiences which started us laughing.

We are now starting to talk about accidents—people getting killed—blood.

Ruby is really rapping about everything—her and her boyfriend—each experience is funny.

When someone would make a statement each one of us would pause (thinking to themselves), laughs or smiles to themselves remembering.

Vic is the person with the questions.

We all get along very well and have different backgrounds. This is good because it brings different topics for discussion.

Nothing that we have or are talking about has been the same.

Tim is more or less the spokesman.

Pam
April 29

Tim is not here. We decided we will have to meet outside of class to get done what needs to be done.

Ruby had to leave; she is sick.

There is not total involvement today. Vic seems like he's on another trip, he keeps looking around the room.

Louise's father might be able to get materials for us.

Carl is tapping his feet. Linda keeps pushing her hair back.

Without Tim, the group is noticeably incomplete.

There seems to be a general feeling of sleepiness or tiredness.

The subject changes to cops and their personalities.

No one is sure exactly what we are going to do.

We decided to write a script for our presentation.

It seems like the group is trying to be involved but would rather rap about other things.

Vic seems to be falling asleep.

The topic changes to the draft and Vic says he's classified I-A, but not for long.

Carl
May 6

This is around our fourth meeting. We began discussing our cube, how we're going to build it. Tim isn't here yet, neither is Ruby. It seems like our group is a little dead. We decided upon a time and place to meet. Wait! Tim just walked into the room. Now the group seems fairly lively. Everybody seems to be taking part. We just voted Warren in our group. Deep blue color for our cube. Tim decided on an outrageous ending. Carl committing suicide, then everybody seemed to dig on that idea. Somebody brought up the date we are going to give our presentation. Tim seemed a little worried about getting finished in time.

Addition by Tim

I'm really proud of our group. In my last group I dictated too much. No one ever disagreed with me. Our group now is different though. I suggested everyone think of what they would really like to say and do. This makes participation great. We don't have one deadhead in the whole group. Whatever happens, I will be satisfied, at least it was all of us doing our damndest to give a creative and uniquely interesting presentation.

Ruby
May 13

Tim is always the first person to start the conversation. Louise went out and priced some wood that we will be using in our presentation. We have decided to paint the boards florescent blue. We have a very enthusiastic group here; our suggestions are really wild. I don't want to write too much about the presentation because we want to surprise you. O.K.?

Tim is the one who seems to be making out the script. We're throwing in our comments and funny suggestions. We seem to disagree a little on certain lines we are each to say; but decided and used the democratic method. Tim got a little tired of both writing the script and figuring out what to say; so Pam is now writing and Tim is the dictator.

We're all laughing because Tim is trying to demonstrate how I'm supposed to be seductive with Carl; and Tim just doesn't seem to understand that the waste paper basket he's using to sit on is going to leave him any minute and he's going to land on the floor. Tim really gets excited when involved with something like this—I say this because I've observed him when I was in Group I last time. Tim's a very outspoken person; I think that's great.

We all helped suggest one another's lines that are the basis for our presentation.

The best thing about this group is that everyone puts in a great deal of participation and no one was left out.

We're trying to be very realistic as to what we say.

It's 1:00 now. Time sure did fly today, but that's because we were having fun.

Tim: This is by far the best observation and feelings in any of the two groups I've been in. I'm not jazzed though with so much of me. Next meeting I think I'll do the diary so everyone else can have a better chance. I think I'm a little too dominant.

What is your reaction to Groups IV and V? What feelings do they send to you? Are they communicating well? Are they helping each other? Could you suggest anything which would help them to do the job more effectively? Which of these groups would you choose to be in? Why?

PARTICIPATING IN A GROUP

We have been through a lot of "heavy" theory and "on-paper" interaction and analysis. It is now time to put yourself into the situation.

For this purpose your instructor will divide you into small groups where you can develop your own helping-communicating culture and put into practice your own ideas about getting along with peers.

As your turn comes around, you will want to write your observation of what goes on in your group. One person at a time is usually enough for this job. But a group without some observer is "flying blind" and may easily get off course or run into a tall building.

To help you do this job of observing, you may want to refer to the appendix for some hints on how and what to observe as well as suggestions on recording your observations. It is essential that you develop your own style, but at the same time your reports will need to include aspects of the group processes which are important. Your group is the best judge of whether or not your record is a realistic and helpful one.

DRAWING CONCLUSIONS:

Now you have experienced group involvement directly as well as read about it. And you have read about and shared your ideas about interacting with your peers in other types of encounters. The next step is to move towards some conclusions. In taking this step, you attempt to form a closure—but not a complete closure—in the pattern of ideas which you have collected about peers. This means that you will want to move towards organizing your ideas, closing the spaces between them, and weaving together the loose ends. In this way a more closely knit pattern of ideas will be formed, but not a pattern which is tightly *closed* and can never be modified.

The following questions may be helpful in attempting to move towards this closure, but do not limit yourself to these questions alone:

1. Which peer groups do you spend most of your time with?
2. In which groups is life the richest and most meaningful to you?
3. To which groups do you go to form close emotional relationships?
4. To which do you go to "straighten out your head"?
5. Which groups, if any, do you avoid?
6. How would you feel about being with Joe, Sylvia, Randy, and Janie of Chapter 1 as a group? Which ones of them would you choose to be with as individuals? Which would you avoid? Why?
7. If you could design your own group of peers—the best one you could imagine—what would it be like? Describe it in a short paragraph.

RELATIONSHIPS WITHIN YOUR SELF

3

INTRODUCTION

In the last chapter you read and rapped about your peers and your feelings and reactions to them. You also worked together with other students, and you got to experience the pleasures and problems which develop when people are involved with each other. As you became involved, did you develop any new feelings or insights about yourself? Often we do see ourselves in the others we associate with. They act as a mirror which reflects us and gives us a new perspective on what we really are like.

In this chapter you will turn your focus from your peers to your self. This is really not a radical shift in emphasis: You will still use the mirror, but you will want to get at more than the reflection. You will want to find out as much about your self as you can.

Finding out about your self will not always seem completely groovy; sometimes it will be very painful, and you'll want to forget the whole scene. If you stick with it, however, you may develop some new insights about your self—insights which can be very helpful in making your life a richer experience than it was before you began to explore your self.

These kinds of insights may be what the four students in chapter 1 were looking for. Keep them in mind as you go through your exploration. They may become part of the mirror which reflects you.

WHAT IS THE SELF?

Structure and Operation of the Self

Each person is unique, and yet people have many things in common with each other. That aspect of us which determines our uniqueness as individuals is called our *self*, our personality, but we all share in common the fact that each of us is a unique self. No one of us is, or can be, just like someone else. Hence the self is both a distinguishing factor—a factor which helps us to be uniquely identified—and a unifying factor—one which unites us with every other individual.

KNOWING ONESELF

But in order to understand the self, we must be aware of certain important ideas. In the first place, no one can completely know himself. This may be illustrated by the accompanying diagram (Fig. 3-1).

Section 1; *KIO*, represents those things which the individual knows about himself which are also known, or could be known, to anyone who associates with him. These are the things which the individual has shared with others and which others have shared with him. Such shared items might include his name, educational background, parentage, place and date of birth, as well as favorable feelings and reactions which he and his associates have towards each other. Section 2, *KI*, represents those things which the individual, only, knows about himself. This is the secret area of the self. It contains things which the individual will want to hide or at least not share with others. Examples of such items might be sexual feelings and experiences, or negative feelings and attitudes which the individual has towards close associates or members of his family. Section 3, *KO*, represents those things which others, only, know and do not want to share with the individual—perhaps to shield

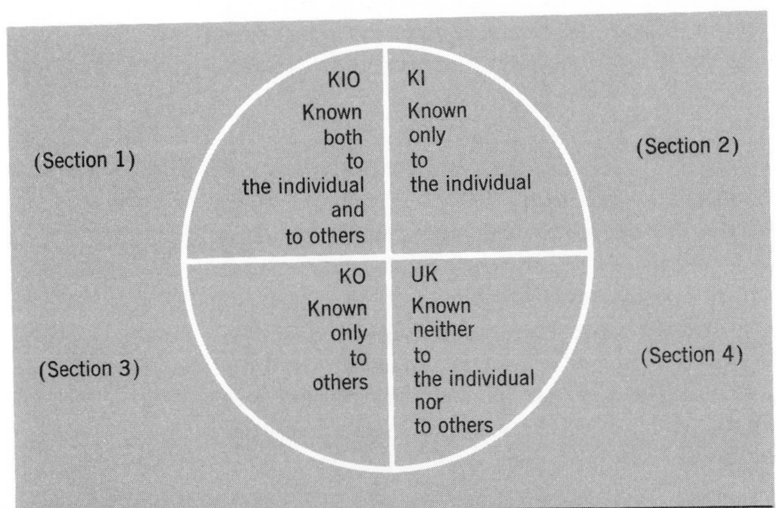

Adapted from the Johari window of Joe Luft and Harry Ingham. See *Group Processes: An Introduction to Group Dynamics*, by Joseph Luft (Palo Alto, Calif.: National Press Book, 1963), p. 11.

FIG. 3–1. THE SELF

him from pain or insult. Examples of this kind of item might include objectionable personal or physical characteristics of the individual: an objectionable voice; bad breath; nervous habits, such as nail-biting or throat-clearing; or a generally sour disposition. Section 4, *UK,* contains things which are consciously known neither by the individual nor by his associates. This section includes forgotten experiences in the past as well as material which is repressed and deals with private areas of experience. The total self is composed of all four of these sections, some consciously known, and some unknown to the individual. He can never know all of his self at one time.

THE STRUCTURE OF THE SELF

The second idea of which we must be aware is that the self is not rigidly determined or structured. It can be changed. Items which are contained in one of the four sections may, through psychotherapy, become known to a psychiatrist and eventually known to the individual himself, thus moving from *UK* to *KIO*. Also, the individual may feel guilty about some items in *KIO* and may repress them, thereby pushing them into *UK*. The four sections of the self are therefore not fixed in content, size, or importance, and the divisions between the sections are permeable; that is, items may be transferred through these divisions from one section to another.

THE SELF CONCEPT

If now we combine *KIO* and *KI*, we have all those aspects of the self of which the individual is aware; we call this combination the *self-concept*. The way the self-concept operates is the third important idea in this discussion.

The self-concept is not the total self, but it is an important aspect of the self for the behavior of individuals is based almost entirely on their perception of things. Therefore, an individual's behavior toward himself is based on how he perceives himself and how he organizes these perceptions—and it is these self perceptions, and his organization of them, which are his self concept. If he considers himself to be ugly, unworthy, and bad, he may be likely to hide, to be self-effacing, and to avoid public attention or self-evaluation. However, he may also try to camouflage his supposed worthlessness with an air of bravado and extroversion. In either case it is his self-concept—the way he perceives himself—which directs his behavior. The differences in the type of behavior are not so much due to differences in self-concept as to the style of mechanisms which the individual uses to adjust to the frustration implicit in seeing himself in negative ways. He may have learned early in life that he could more skillfully use one style of adjustment mechanisms than another, and therefore, he unconsciously selects this style for his acting out. Hence the two different behaviors—hiding and bravado—may stem from the same low self-concept.

THE EFFECT OF FEELINGS AND VALUES ABOUT ONESELF

It is obvious from the preceding discussion, that the components of the self-concept—the items of *KIO* and *KI* of the diagram—are not just factual material. This brings us to the fourth important idea about the self: Not only are facts closely associated with feelings and values, these feelings and values are the most important factor in determining how we act and behave. It is really not so important, as far as influencing my behavior is concerned, whether I am, in reality, tall or short, thin or fat, old or young, college graduate or non-college graduate, married or single, homosexual or heterosexual, black or white, Protestant or Catholic. What is important is the value I give to having any one of these characteristics as opposed to the other, and how I feel about having it. Such feelings and values are often so powerful that they can actually distort or overbalance what might commonly be considered the accepted truth. For instance, consider a female, who is five feet four inches tall, and weighs 115 lbs., a weight which appears to other people to be very attractively distributed. However, she may consider herself short, fat, and generally unattractive. She may therefore avoid the beach, where her figure will be in view, wear badly-fitting clothes, and torture herself with an unreasonable reducing diet, denying herself gastronomic pleasures as well as many forms of social interaction.

THE EFFECT OF THE "UNKNOWN" SECTIONS OF THE SELF

It is important at this point to consider a fifth idea about the self. While the self-concept is most *directly* responsible for our behavior, the other two sections of the self—*KO* and *UK*—can have a powerful indirect influence on behavior through their ability to change the self-concept itself. If people think of me as repulsive and shun me, even if it is because of characteristics I have of which I am not conscious, it will certainly cause my self-concept to be affected. I may not know that I have bad breath, but I do know I am shunned. A sexual experience in early childhood, which is now repressed and therefore not known to me, may prevent me from having enjoyable sexual experiences now, an occurrence which will affect my self-concept. These unknown parts of the self *do* affect behavior, largely indirectly, by means of their influences on the conscious areas of the self.

The sixth important point about the self comes to us in the form of two very crucial questions: How can the self, through the self-concept, be developed and changed in desirable directions? How can we become what we want to be?

In order to do justice to this discussion, we must recognize that we are not born with a self-concept. At birth the human infant doesn't really have a self at all. We denote this by referring to an infant as "it". Very quickly material in *KO* develops as the baby begins to make its presence felt. From *KO*, with the efforts of the family, *KIO* begins to emerge. We must remember that this development is difficult. At first the infant does not even know how to distinguish its body from its mother's body, much less any of its more abstract attributes. As *KIO* develops factually, values quickly follow. One needs acceptance in order to be warm, so one learns which acts are acceptable and which acts are equally desirable to us but are not acceptable to others. Therefore, one learns to suppress consciously and then to repress unconsciously, and in so doing the material in *KI* and *UK* is developed. The crucial points here are that the self-concept is learned, not genetically inherited; and that this learning takes place in a social context—it is learned from others by interacting with them in various ways.

Furthermore, many of these patterns of interaction are largely beyond the conscious control of the infant or even of the small child. Our feeling that we—our *selves*—are unchangeable is due largely to the social straight-jacketing into which we are born, rather than to inherent rigidity within ourselves. Therefore the crucial factor for producing behavioral change and learning in order to become what we want to be is to seek for more growth-producing

—less rigid—social contexts in which to be involved and thus change and enhance our self-concept, and correspondingly make our behavior more satisfying and enriching. For those people whose self-concepts are painted in negative colors, this means we must call on the other pigments of the psychic palette, which will generally be found in *KO* and *UK*, and are probably tightly locked in there. To release them requires an atmosphere where camouflage can be gradually removed and privacy gently and gradually reduced. In such an atmosphere, self-disclosure will develop, and as the individual discloses himself to others, he will learn from them positive things about himself which were formerly stored in *KO*. As this process continues, he and others will also gradually open *UK*. In these two sections positive facts and values will begin to emerge, and the permeability of the compartments of the self can be restored so that the energy used to keep them impermeable, or permeable in only one direction, can be used more fully for the creative enjoyment of a self-fulfilling life.

THE SELF-IDEAL

We are now ready to consider the seventh important idea about the self. This idea has to do with what is called the self-ideal, that which the individual would like to become, or achieve, in the future. This concept is closely related to the sixth point—how to facilitate desirable changes in the self. It might be considered a facilitating agent—something which, correctly developed, makes the change easier. But it may also be an inhibiting agent—something which incorrectly developed, makes the change more difficult.

If the self-ideal is clear, realistic, and not too far from possible achievement, then it may be a facilitating agent. If it is vague, unreal, or far beyond what can be expected, then it may inhibit change in the self in any desirable way. The self-ideal starts to form in childhood, and is strongly influenced by "significant others" who are present at that time. The competence of these "others"—or their lack of it—can have a strong influence on what the child wants to become or fears he will become.

For example, a child whose parents are effective in living their own lives, as well as supportive of him in his efforts to achieve, will probably develop a clear, realistic self-ideal—one which he can reasonably expect to achieve. A child whose parents are not effective in life, and for this reason have negative attitudes, and are also repressive with respect to his efforts to succeed, will probably have only the vaguest kind of self-ideal or one which cannot be achieved. For example, he may be a 140-pound youth who wants to be an All-America tackle, or a mathematically inept student who wants to be a research scientist. In general, only if such a child finds his competence model and support elsewhere, can he be expected to form a positive self-ideal and become what he wants to be.

In summary, everybody has a self. It can never be completely known, but it is always possible to know it better than we know it currently. As we get to know our self better, we will find that the self and its parts are not fixed or rigidly set. The self is actively directed by a self-concept—the way the individual sees himself—and this self-concept is influenced by feelings and values even more than by facts. The self-concept is also indirectly influenced by the unknown and subconscious aspects of the self. Hence in order to change the self the divisions between conscious and unconscious sections must be kept permeable; in other words, subject to the transmission of items from one section to another. It is also important for the individual to seek social contexts where he can share disclosures about himself with others as well as to form a realistic self-ideal with the help of the signicant others in his life.

HOW DOES THE SELF DEVELOP?

In spite of all the pleasures and enjoyment we experience in life, one of the most illuminating ways to analyze our behavior and understand how our self develops is in terms of the frustrations we experience. We mean by frustration any interruption of a particular act which stops us from achieving the goal we had in mind.

There are three ways in which frustration usually comes about: (1) *by delay,* (2) *by blocking,* and (3) *by conflict.* Waiting for a letter or phone call from someone special is frustration by delay. All forms of undesirable waiting can usually be classified as this kind of frustration. Frustration by blocking is sometimes deliberate, as shown by the football player who uses and experiences blocking as an essential part of the game. However, we are often blocked in life by obstacles not under our control—by lack of money, by the color of our skin, or by our lack of ability in school when we seek a job. The third type of frustration—that caused by conflict—is much more complicated than the other two forms of frustration. The four ways in which conflict may develop are described below.

APPROACH-APPROACH CONFLICT. ++

This form of conflict is one in which we are blocked in choosing which of two desirable objects we want. The conflict arises because we cannot have both of them, so one must be rejected. Examples of this are choosing a husband from two very attractive men; choosing one of two equally delicious desserts; or choosing to attend one of two equally exciting athletic events which occur at the same time. This type of conflict is usually resolved by moving closer to the choice of one of the alternatives. When one of two desirable alternatives is brought closer to us, it usually becomes considerably more or less desirable, and therefore the conflict is broken.

AVOIDANCE-AVOIDANCE CONFLICT. ––

In this form of conflict we are faced with the choice of one of two alternatives, *neither* of which is attractive to us. However, the situation is such that one alternative *must* be chosen. The situation of the college student who does not like to study but must maintain a certain grade-point average in order to avoid the draft is typical of this type of conflict. Another example is the voter who must choose between two equally drab candidates, or the woman who feels that her last chance to avoid being an old maid is to marry a man she considers rather repugnant and unloved. The usual attempted response to this type of conflict is escape, if that outlet is at all possible. The student may dodge both college and the draft by going to Canada. The voter may not vote, or may write in a candidate. The single woman may seek means other than marriage to find rewarding social relationships.

APPROACH-AVOIDANCE CONFLICT. ±

This type of conflict develops due to the fact that an object of choice has at the same time both desirable and undesirable characteristics. The desire of a child to pet a dog of which he is afraid is an example of this type of conflict, as is a man who wants a life companion in marriage but doesn't want to be tied down, or a girl who wants to marry a particular man but does not want to be associated with his family. This type of conflict can only be overcome if one of the two sets of characteristics—positive or negative—can be seen to clearly outweigh the other, so that a choice or a rejection is clearly indicated as being the desirable alternative.

DOUBLE APPROACH-AVOIDANCE CONFLICT. ±±

This type of conflict is usually the most frustrating type. A girl with two lovers, both of whom are asking to marry her, finds herself in this situation: Each man has desirable characteristics; one is handsome, but the other is wealthy. Handsome Harry has a very over-protective mother. Roger Moneybags insists on living in what she perceives as a very undesirable location. What can she do? Of course, a third alternative is to marry someone else, but these two men are far more attractive than anyone else she could imagine. Only if personal attractiveness can outweigh an undesirable family, or if money can outweigh location, can she solve this dilemma—unless she discovers some new qualities about one of the men which throw the balance clearly for or against him.

We all know that frustration is far too upsetting a phenomenon to be experienced without any reaction. Therefore, whenever we experience any of these frustrations, we tend to react with one of the three types of *behavioral mechanisms* described below.

Defensive behavior. In this type of adjustment to frustration, we employ some means to defend or protect ourselves against the discomfort of the frustration.

One of these mechanisms is *rationalization.* In this mechanism the frustrated person attempts to explain his inability by means of some other reason which sounds better to his ego. For instance, a boy who does not make the football team may say that he didn't want to play football anyway. He would rather save himself for basketball or be free to have more fun with his friends at times when the team will be practicing. A girl who wasn't invited to the prom by a particular boy may say that she really didn't want to go with him anyway, and would rather stay home and watch her favorite television program. Furthermore, she might say that the band that was going to play for the prom was lousy, and besides she could have much better entertainment on TV or listening to her stereo.

A second defensive type of adjustment is *projection.* A person who uses this mechanism attributes to someone else feelings, attitudes, or motives which are really his own and are probably not the feelings, attitudes, or motives of the other person. For example, a student who cheats on an exam may use as his excuse that "everyone else cheats anyway," or a person who falls in love may say "You made me love you. I didn't want to do it," in the attempt to excuse his intense feelings for the other person.

A third mechanism of the defensive type is *identification.* In this case the frustrated person loses his frustration with his own inability by identifying with a group or another person who is successful. For example, a parent who is an immigrant from another country and has had little education may compensate for his lack of literacy by identifying with his child and feeling pride in every step of the child's progress in school, or a boy who is crippled and thus cannot compete in athletics may become strongly identified with the whole group of athletes at his school and lose his frustration by following every minute of each athletic contest.

A fourth form of defensive adjustment is *emotional isolation.* In this type of mechanism the person who feels inadequate in dealing with conflict, tension, or even love, adjusts by removing all emotion from his reactions and simply approaching each situation of potential conflict in a strictly intellectual way. He says "I understand your hostility towards me. Therefore I feel no pain from it!" He always understands everything. He has no intense feelings and does not think they are necessary. He always talks softly and never "lets himself go." In this way he defends himself against the frustration and damage which an emotional explosion or "flood" would do to his social relationships.

Avoidance or Withdrawal. In this second general type of adjustment to frustration, we usually avoid the frustration or find some means to withdraw from the whole conflict scene.

The most obvious kind of avoidance is simple or *direct avoidance.* Thus, the person who feels inadequate with the opposite sex simply avoids all members of that sex. The person who is frustrated in school drops out and avoids all contact with educational institutions.

A second means of withdrawal is *regression*. An individual who is frustrated withdraws from the present frustrating scene to a past social context where he felt more secure. A child at the age of six or seven may therefore resort to thumb-sucking or bed-wetting when frustrated, or a grown man may throw a temper tantrum and yell at his associates when frustrated—as he used to do as a child with his parents.

A third form of withdrawal is *fantasy*. When faced with the frustration of loneliness we often resort to daydreams (or even night dreams) of association with pleasant companions, or if we are poor and need money, food, clothes, and the like, we may dream—with the help of our television—of a more affluent life. The unloved person may dream of his lovers, the unsuccessful person may dream of his conquests, and the ugly person may dream of being beautiful.

The fourth form of withdrawal is a very complicated one, of which there are many perplexing examples. It is puzzling often because it seems that the individual has no control over it. This is the *flight into illness*. This is the case in which a child gets sick at school time, but never on Saturday. A tooth stops aching as the dentist's office is approached. One becomes fatigued and sleepy whenever a difficult job must be done. A person forgets to do a disagreeable task or keep an appointment which will result in conflict or embarrassment. A man develops ailments such as asthma, eczema, or hay fever (which makes him dependant, incapacitated or "explains" his unattractiveness to others); blindness—partial or total; paralysis of certain kinds; deafness; dizziness. All of these reactions may be used—unconsciously—as a means of escaping from coping with conflict, anxiety and frustration. Dual personalities, amnesia, compulsions to act in a particular way, and obsessive ideas from which we "cannot escape", are also mechanisms used to withdraw from rational coping with the problems of life. One must continually keep in mind that these flights into seeming organic disabilities are not consciously chosen by the person. Therefore, asking him to stop only makes the flight more intense and adds insuit to injury.

Aggressive Behavior. People who use this type of reaction to frustration do so by venting emotion or action towards some object. This object may or may not be the object which is really causing the frustration.

The simplest form of aggressive behavior is direct *extra-punitive behavior.* The person who is blocked physically or verbally assaults the person or thing which is blocking him. We kick at a biting dog. We punish an unruly child. We attack someone who invades the privacy of our home. We argue with the policeman or teacher who has treated us unreasonably.

A second form of aggression is *intro-punitive behavior,* in which we do not attack the external offender, but rather blame ourselves. The student says, "I am stupid. I deserved to fail," or the driver says " I was careless. I deserve to get the traffic ticket."

A third form of aggressive behavior is *displacement.* In this form of behavior we are overly aggressive, but not to the cause of our frustration. The student who needs very much to succeed in school may take his reprimand from the teacher quietly, and then punch one of his friends in the nose to "let off stream." A girl who has split up with her boyfriend may rant and rail at her parents.

One interesting form of displacement is so-called *juvenile delinquency.* Here an oppressed group of adolescents may beat out their frustrations by destructive behavior against property of persons who had nothing to do with their oppression and who may, in fact, be actively working in their behalf.

Sometimes feelings of aggression are *compensated* for by letting these feelings out in a non-destructive way. One who feels physically pent up may let out his feelings by chopping wood or by indulging in contact sports or other forms of athletics. These feelings may even be *sublimated* by directing them to a more inactive level physically, but one which still releases much of the pent-up emotion. Such activities might be painting, plastic art, writing poetry or fiction, or dramatics.

Finally, some of us use *reaction-formation* as a way of dealing with our feelings of aggression. Here we may be overly considerate to someone whom we feel we *should* love but whom we actually hate: for example, a child or parent. We may be overly quiet or polite to the teacher or the policeman who is reprimanding us. This display of reversed emotion is acceptable, and yet it does provide us with an emotional outlet.

In conclusion, it is important to understand that most of us use a variety of mechanisms to deal with the problems of life. The mechanisms are generally *not* maladjustments and only become so when they tend to incapacitate us. Some mechanisms—fantasy, for example—can be very creative and can often be cultivated to great advantage.

The list of mechanisms above by which we may adjust to frustration is by no means complete. However, it is at least a start in understanding how we come to be the kind of self we are, and how this self develops. If we are to become what we *want* to be, this knowledge is very important. But it must be "understood" with the feelings and emotions as well as with the mind. As you go through the applications which follow, you may begin to develop this kind of emotional understanding along with the factual understanding of your self which you already have.

APPLYING WHAT YOU'VE LEARNED ABOUT THE SELF

These applications are intended to show how the theory, which has just been presented, can be applied in specific situations. It is divided into four sections. The first part deals with students' attempts to tell the psychological stories of their lives. The second deals with students' attempts to interpret their personalities. The third part shows how stories written by students can lead to knowledge about their selves. The last part shows how a mirror can be used to reflect more than just physical features.

DESCRIBING THE SELF

The autobiographies which follow were written by two lower division college students, *W* and *X*, who were enrolled in a psychology class. They were attempting to tell the psychological story of their lives. Read through these reports carefully and ask yourself the following questions:

1. What facts does each student mention about himself which would fall under Section *KIO* of the Self diagram? (See Figure 3–1)
2. Which facts would fall under *KI*?
3. As we said in the beginning of the chapter, we are not aware of items in *KO* and *UK*. However, can you suggest from these autobiographies facts about these students which might conceivably fall under *KO* and *UK*?

4. Show by drawing a self-diagram (as in Figure 3–1 on page 45) the relative size of the four sections for each student. Give your evidence for this.
5. Indicate the typical types of frustration and the style of adjustment mechanisms used by each student.
6. Who are the "significant others" in the lives of each of these students? Who are the "significant others" in your life? What influences do these "others" have in your life?
7. What differences do you find between the self-concepts and ideal selves for each of these students? What differences do you find between your self-concept and self-ideal?
8. Write a thumbnail sketch of each of these students and inindicate their obvious characteristics.
9. Answer questions 1–7 for the four students in chapter 1. How would they compare to Students W and X?
10. Compare the two students' personalities. Which one is most like you? Why?
11. Discuss your answer to question 10 in light of the autobiography which you wrote earlier.

Autobiography
Written by Student W

The first psychological experience I remember is when I was about four years old. I spent the Christmas with my uncle and aunt. On Christmas Eve my aunt was getting ready to give me a bath and the water in the tub was still hot when there was a knock on the door. I was nude, but my aunt told me to go open the door. This wasn't unusual because we lived in a small community and everyone knew everyone else. I opened the door and Santa Clause was standing there. I don't know whether I was frightened or excited, but I ran back to my aunt and almost fell in the tub of hot water. This episode has left a very warm feeling in my heart. But my Christmases were not always happy. From about the ages 9–14 I visited my grandmother during Christmas and she had a special knack of making my Christmases unhappy. Every Christmas she would do or say something to spoil my day. I don't think she realized she was doing this.

The Christmases I spent with my mother (6–8 and 15–present) were and still are happy, but they could be better because my mother has to work; there's no real family togetherness. I think this has had a psychological effect on me in that now I am determined to give my family (husband and children) the kind of Christmases that I've never had.

From about the age of four (about the farthest back I can remember) to about the age of nine, was one of the happiest periods in my life. I would sit out on the high wall in front of our house every afternoon and wait for my mother and the lady we live with. This lady was my grandfather's second wife and I considered her my grandmother. I would wait for them to get off the bus. When they arrived, I would run to meet them and ask what they brought me. Sometimes I didn't get anything, but most of the time I did, because my grandmother worked in the delicatessen. Sitting waiting for my mother and grandmother every day made me very talkative and they were always ready and willing to listen to what I had to say.

But when I was in the fifth grade all of this began to change. My mother began to feel that my grandmother (father's mother—my parents are divorced) could do a better job of raising me than she could. I had never liked living with my grandmother before, but I was going to put up a big effort to like my grandmother more since I had to live with her now. It worked for about a week and then my grandmother started making me do extra work, and she and my sister (my sister has lived with her all her life) would never listen to anything I had to say. I put up with this for about three years, but what I didn't know was that it all was going to get worse. About the beginning of my fourth year, everything started to get extremely bad. My grandmother started making all sorts of accusations about me. I matured faster than my sister (she's older than me) and I developed more than she. At first my grandmother started talking to me about boys. Then she started accusing me of letting boys be overly familiar with me. Then every time something in the house got broken, I was accused of breaking it. She would argue at me if I arrived home five minutes later than my sister. When I wanted to visit a friend (I was 14 years old) who lived only two or three blocks away, I was permitted to stay just one hour and I "had" to go every place with either her or my sister. These things made me very unhappy. I would cry a lot (never around her). When my father came home to visit (he lived in Washington, D.C.) I would never do anything with them, because I felt like a stranger. I would go in another room alone, because no matter how much I tried, I could never be happy with them. My father made things worse. He was my grandmother's "baby," so that meant everything had to be done extra well. To top things off, my grandmother would talk on the telephone and say mean things about me and always compare me to my sister. I was always the worst.

During all this time, I wanted to tell my mother my problems, but she and I had lost our mother-daughter relationship. She had moved to Nevada. One day my grandmother really got to me. So I wrote my mother a letter but instead of telling her all I've told you, I told her that she didn't want me, that she just wanted me to clean for her and I said a lot of other things. I regretted this letter after I had mailed it. I regretted it more after my mother answered it, because I had really hurt her.

I wrote that letter in early spring and in early fall my mother came to get me, but in between that time, things became even harder and more accusations were put on me plus the constant reminder of the letter. But, worst of all, my grades were being affected. School had been in session about a month when my mother came to get me. In the meantime, I was in danger of failing all my classes, even P.E. I had been an honor student all through school and I had just been put in the National Honor Society the year before.

When my mother took me back to Nevada, my life began to look brighter again. My mother trusted me. She never accused me of anything. She treated me as a person should be treated. My grades started coming up to par.

But the experience of the past four years had left a scar on me. I could not and still cannot talk to my mother. I'm no longer talkative. I'm very shy and where I could once make friends very easily, I can no longer do that. I'm afraid that they're invading my privacy.

In the past six years my psychological life has been up and down, but nothing has made a big impression.

My psychological experiences have made me determined to get a good education (good education usually means no work on holidays) and work hard to make my marriage last, because there's no substitute to being raised by one's own parents.

Autobiography
Written by Student X

My early youth has had a tremendous influence upon my life. I feel that it has shaped my whole outlook on life and the way I act in it. The now trivial problems, my many varied experiences and adventures, and the happiness and general well-roundedness of my childhood has made me into what I consider a person who can someday be a responsible person with a challenging career.

My first few years of life are very vague to me. Although I can catch snatches of it at intervals now and then, they are not significant enough for me to perceive what, if any, influence those years had upon me. Some of these recollections I can remember are of being with my best friend (Joe) and having a babysitter take care of us. Both of our mothers worked. This was the reason for the babysitter. Both Joe and I hated this setup although, naturally, there was nothing we could do about it. I know probably that this has influenced my latter life in some ways, although I could only think of one which would be connected with it—my hatred for an authoritarian adult. My childish reasoning told me that this adult was not related to me, so why should he (she) tell me what to do? I would feign sickness or some poor excuse, just so I would not have to do what I was told. All through life I have hated adults who, whether right or wrong, would press their power down my throat. I would argue, even though practical sense told me that most adults will not give ground to a "child" no matter what. I now realize that at eighteen most people consider me an adult. So now I do not run across this problem so much, but for many years it was a very big "hang-up" for me.

In the first three years of school, I had many accidents. In kindergarten, I flew off the slide into the pavement; result—home for a few weeks and the warm security of mother's arms. The next year proved just as fruitful—I was hit by a car. Although the injuries were rather minor (a cut-up head and a badly bruised and cut right arm), it brought me back home again. The next year I slipped and fell and opened up one of the previous lacerations in my head—again the security of home. To call me accident prone is a rather large understatement. Every cut and bruise brought the sympathy and security that I felt I so dearly lacked. Although there was much love in my home, I still felt I needed a handicap to get me on par with the two older children. All through my childhood and early teens I seemed to lose enough blood to supply the Red Cross for months. This, at least, I felt, brought me sympathy. As I got older, I realized that my efforts only brought me self-pity. But this did not stop me. In football, during high school, whenever I failed, it was because of my "injuries." In fact, for almost all of my failures, it was because of some uncontrollable injury. Although I realize now that everyone gives himself reasons for his failures, I have always felt that I overdid it. I still give myself excuses for my failures, although I must say they are more rational than in the previous years.

My home life has been always rather happy. Although my parents are now divorced, they supplied a relatively happy home until their separation. My mother has given me my greatest, or rather best, habits. She loved to read. She has passed this love on to me through the great quantity of literature which has always been prevalent at my house. My strange curiosity that there is a reason for anything that happens, can also be attributed to my mother. Although my mother and I do argue quite violently quite often, I would attribute this, as my father has mentioned to me, to our personalities being very much alike, rather than anything from my childhood. My mother and I will only take so much from one another; we will argue, neither one of us giving any ground to the other. Although this has provided many difficulties it has also given to both of us a very deep and meaningful friendship.

My father and I are now close as friends. When he lived at home, we were not too close. He and my older brother were and have always been very close. Being that my older brother was the oldest child, this could be the reason for their closeness. It seemed whenever there was to be work (yard) done around the house, I ended up doing it. Although I loved to do it at the time, the noncooperation from the rest of my family has left me as a very lazy (mentally) person when it comes to yard work.

My older brother and I have never really gotten along together. When I was younger and he was living at home, he would use me as a punching bag at his convenience. Believe me, I am not complaining about this. It taught me how to take punches (although I have never really known how to fight back). But it did give me very deep hatred for him, which I try to rationalize, but I realize it is impossible. I have, and I probably always will have, this hatred which will never be erased. I must also add that it taught me something else. I used to beat up on my younger brother, but this brought me many guilt feelings: I am now to him just about the opposite person my older brother was to me. I suppose these guilt feelings arise from the anxieties I got when I hit him. I suppose I do not hit him because I am trying to act out the role of the older brother that I always secretly desired to have my older brother play. Also, I am afraid that if I did hit him, I would be the same type of person my brother is. This is something I surely do not desire. When he is home, I am polite to him, although it is more of an ignorance. I do this mainly for my mother, for I have no intention of ever seeing him when I leave home. My sister and I have always gotten along. Our relationship is rather close, or rather, as normal brother and sister.

I mentioned a friend (Joe) of mine earlier. We grew up together from the time of our first step to the present. I must mention that this is the most invaluable friendship I have ever or will ever have. Naturally, we went through puberty and all its difficulties together. Our personalities and goals are nowhere near alike. Our actions and reactions are likewise. I have always told Joe that if we had not grown up together, I could not stand him. We both have our many faults, but our long lasting friendship has made their interference nil. Both of us have always used each other for whipping posts. Whenever we are angry for any reason over anything, we can cuss at each other and have no fear of the loss of this friendship. This is the greatest thing in the world for both of us. Without this close friendship, I know that it would have been very difficult growing up. It has brought us over many problems, and I will always be thankful for it.

Now comes my greatest joy—girls. From the time I was in fourth grade, I have been interested (very) in the opposite sex. Up until high school, I had many girls as friends. When high school hit, I hit at the books. At least for the first two years I did. It seems as though all of my friends through the seventh and eighth grades were having a contest to see who was getting the most A's. Naturally, this left me sort of out in right field. So, all through the summer before high school, I mentally told myself that I would study hard. This mental preparation paid off well. Going into my junior year I had a 3.88 average, well within the top five percent of my class. This ended when I met a girl I went with one and one-half years. Her parents were divorced. I suppose both of us were looking for security and warmth, for whenever either one of us had an argument with our parent, we would go to the other. Since we lived just a few houses from each other, it made this possible. Because of our yearning for someone, we became very close, and as far as I could see then, very much in love. Since both of us were rather young at the time, we had not experienced too much the joy of dating others. Consequently, whenever one of us was away for a while from the other, we would (since we were going steady) "cheat" on the other while just as likely the one at home would do the same thing. I realize now that both of us were looking for security, or rather a home away from home, so we could have a stable base to go out into the world. It gave us the security of having someone to love and be loved by whenever we failed outside. We broke up quite often, so we both had plenty of opportunities to date others without guilt feelings. I cannot say that this relationship was meaningless, at the time. I now feel both of us needed it very much. And I realize now just what is needed for a close relationship. Of course, I learned quite a bit (like arguing—which will probably be quite invaluable in marriage), but most important, I feel, I am much more mature because of this relationship with this person.

Now that I am entering my higher education, I realize the importance of my childhood. Although I know that I am not near my maturity yet, I feel my background has made me a stable enough person to realize my goals, strive for them, and hopefully, reach them.

GAINING INSIGHT FROM THE INCOMPLETE SENTENCE TEST

The materials which follow have to do with the Incomplete Sentence Test. This test consists of fifty incomplete sentences which the student completes with the first thought that comes into his mind. He then uses these spontaneous responses to get a clearer picture of his self and attempts to report what he finds as completely and objectively as he can.

STEP 1

Look at the Incomplete Sentence Test for person 81. You will notice that the items of the test, itself, are not in parentheses. The part of each item in parentheses is the response which was made to the item by person 81.

Incomplete Sentence Test (Form IC–2) for Person 81[1]

Complete these sentences to express how you really feel. Work rapidly and try to be fully frank. Sometimes a word will suffice to complete your idea; sometimes a phrase or a sentence will best convey your thought. Try to reveal as much of your feelings as you can.

1. I like (to be with girls who are good looking.)
2. At night (I like a nice warm bed.)
3. Children (are sometimes enjoyable and often times not.)
4. School is (the basis for a full and complete life.)
5. Other people (are funny to watch.)
6. I hate (a know-it-all.)
7. I wish (I had a good job to make more money.)
8. My mother (is sometimes unreasonable.)
9. Men are (great liars.)
10. My life (is going to be very successful.)
11. I need (someone.)
12. The best (way to succeed is to try hard.)
13. My work (gives me a pain.)
14. When I'm alone (I wish I weren't.)
15. Marriage is (great when you are prepared for it.)
16. My health (is great.)
17. What annoys me is (fat women.)
18. My father (is a hard worker.)
19. Sexual relationships (excite me.)
20. My ambition is (to make a million.)
21. The worst (girls smoke.)
22. Studying (is lots of times hard.)
23. I avoid (embarrassing situations.)
24. My nerves (are easily shot.)
25. I consider myself to be (a good painter.)
26. Dirty (words.)
27. I fear (dark alleys.)
28. My mind (wanders.)
29. My home (is a wonderful place.)
30. I regret (hurting people.)

---

[1]Reprinted from Leon Gorlow, Erasmus L. Hoch, and Earl F. Telechow, *The Nature of Nondirective Group Psychotherapy: An Experimental Investigation* (New York: Bureau of Publications, Teachers College, Columbia University, 1952) by permission of the authors and publisher.

31. Most women (are nice.)
32. The future (is bright.)
33. As a child, I (played a lot.)
34. What thrills me is (racing cars.)
35. Drinking (is sickening.)
36. My disposition (is normal.)
37. Few people know that I (have ability.)
38. I am proudest of (large crowds.)
39. I get depressed (when things are difficult.)
40. I am closest to (my dad.)
41. People consider me (fun.)
42. I look forward to (art college.)
43. I am ashamed of (some things.)
44. I wish people would (lay off.)
45. My worst fault is (my temper.)
46. I feel (good.)
47. I sometimes think (of embarrassing situations.)
48. My biggest worry (is girls.)
49. My greatest joy (is getting satisfaction.)
50. Secretly (I wish I could move away.)

STEP 2

Now look at the chart for this test, Table 3-1.

TABLE 3-1
CHART OF RESPONSES OF PERSON 81 TO THE INCOMPLETE SENTENCE TEST

Self	Others		Family and Home	Education or School	Job and Work	Things	Past	Future	Blocks	Conflict
10 −	1 +	21 −	2 +	4 +	7 −	2 +	33 +	10 +	12	3
11 −	3 + −	23 −	8 −	22 −	13 −	26? −	1 +	20 +	27	30
14 −	5 +	30 + −	18 +	42 +	2 −	27 −		32 +	26	(29–50)
16 +	6 −	31 +	29 +	2 +		34 +		42 +	35	(17–31)
24 −	8 −	38 +	40 +	1 −		39 −		4 +	43	15?
25 +	9 −	40 +	50 −			3 −			49	8?
28 −	11 +	44 −	4 +			2 +				
36 0	15 +	47 −	2 −							
37 +	17 −	48 −								
41 +	18 +	9 −								
45 −	19 +	9 +								
46 +		2 + −								
5 +										
6 −										
1 0										

You will notice that the items are in columns according to whether they indicate an attitude directed towards (a) the student himself (in the *Self* column); (b) other people (in the *Others* column); (c) family and home; (d) school or education; (e) work or job; (f) material things, not people; (g) events which are now past; (h) events which will not take place until the future; (i) blocked responses, items which give no attitudinal value and (j) conflicts—items which show conflicting attitudes directed towards the same object.

Notice that an item is scored +, if it is a positive reaction (example: "My health is good"); scored − if the reaction is negative (example: "Children are a drag"); scored 0 if the response is neutral (example: "Men are males") or +− if the response is conflicting (example: "My mother is good to me when she isn't scolding").

Notice that items which are put under *Self* must refer directly to the person's attitudes towards himself—for example, "I like people" or "I like to drive fast" do not refer directly to "Self." "People consider me to be handsome" does indicate an attitude toward self. So does "My life is happy."

Notice that blocks are of two kinds—items which are not completed and non-committal items (usually scored 0). The former is usually the more solid of the two blocks.

Notice that the conflicts are of two kinds—those which occur in a single item, as mentioned above, and conflicts between two items (example: "My mother is very loving and kind to me" and "What annoys me is my mother trying to run my affairs").

STEP 3

The following is an interpretation of person 81 based on the information in the chart. This interpretation was done by a student.

No. 81 is a person who directs his thoughts to others when faced with a situation which is open. Of the 22 such questions, he directed only two to himself, but 10 to others. This attraction to others is further evidenced by his need for someone (11) and his wish not to be alone (13). In general, this is a reflection of self-negative feelings as seen in the following items: I need someone when I'm alone I wish I weren't, I avoid embarrassing situations, my nerves are easily shot, my mind wanders, I regret hurting people, I get depressed when things are difficult, I am ashamed of some things, my worst fault is my temper. This shows a definite trend of looking at himself in negative terms. This may have resulted from his poor relationship with his mother who was sometimes unreasonable and in her unreasonableness left her mark on him so that he believes he is no good and lacking in these traits.

His interest in others really creates a conflict for him in that he seeks others and yet he avoids embarrassing situations (23)—which must involve others; he sometimes thinks of embarrassing situations (47), his biggest worry is girls (48), and he wishes people would lay off (44). Evidently he does not succeed in his relations with others without causing embarrassing situations, or losing his temper (45). His success may come in crowds (where he can lose himself) as he is proudest of large crowds (38).

Evidently his present job is not satisfying as he makes two negative references to it, (7, 13) and a questionable reference (12). Yet this does not dim his hopes for the future as evidenced by his "life is to be very successful" (10), "future is bright" (32); "make a million" (20) dampens this view because he must know that this is highly improbable and is therefore negative.

His view of school is positive in that he feels it's the basis for a full and complete life (4), and he's looking forward to his future at art college, although he admits studying is at times hard (22).

He says good things about his father and home.

Some of his troubles in embarrassing situations may come from his contradictory feelings about the female sex. This is brought about by his conflict in his feelings dealing with his family. He says good things about his father (men) and home (18, 29, 40) but has reservations about his mother (8) and contradicts it all when he says he secretly wishes he could leave home. Evidently he has an understanding with his father which he doesn't have with his mother as evidenced by his reaction "he is closest to his dad." But what of his reactions that men are liars—and most women are nice, but he fears girls, and fat women annoy him? It would seem he is quite mixed up in his feelings about men and women and these feelings may have led him into those embarrassing situations where he trusted a man, and then found he couldn't (men are liars), or was afraid of a relationship with a woman and then had a satisfactory experience (most women are nice). It would be interesting to know if his mother was fat—or who in his experience was.

He is non-committal about *who* he needs (11), what kinds of situations are embarrassing (23) and what kinds of satisfaction gives his greatest joy (29).

He has conflicts about his home (50, 29) his feelings about children (3), and men and women, and marriage (15).

STEP 4

Now turn to the Incomplete Sentence Tests for students *Y* and *Z*. Enter their responses on charts like the one used for person 81. (See Table 3-1.)

When you have scored and classified all items, you may have a few which don't seem to fit anywhere. Should they all pertain to one particular area of life, such as "sports," or "religion," make a new column for them. If not, don't put them anywhere, but keep a record of them since they may be needed later.

Now, what would you say were the outstanding characteristics of students Y and Z? In order to make your answer to this question more explicit, consider the following:

1. What facts, mentioned or implied by each student, would fall under each of the four sections of the self diagram: *KIO, KI, KO,* and *UK* (see Figure 3-1)?
2. What type of frustrations does each student typically encounter?
3. What are the most typical adjustment or behavioral mechanisms used by each student?
4. How does each student typically "look at the world": as friendly? as hostile? as neutral? as an object to be studied? as a great unknowable? Other?
5. As in the section on describing the self (pp. 56–57), write a thumbnail sketch of each student, indicating briefly his most outstanding characteristics.
6. Refer back to the four students in chapter 1. Even though you do not actually know these students, can you predict how each one would complete some of the items of the Incomplete Sentence Test? Fill out a test for each of the four—Joe, Sylvia, Randy, and Janie—as completely as you can. How do their responses compare with the responses of Y and Z?

Incomplete Sentence Test
(Form IC-S) for Student Y

Complete these sentences to express how you really feel. Work rapidly and try to be fully frank. Sometimes a word will suffice to complete your idea; sometimes a phrase or a sentence will best convey your thought. Try to reveal as much of your feelings as you can.

1. I like (people.)
2. At night (I sleep.)
3. Children (are beautiful.)
4. School is (good for responsibility.)
5. Other people (never cease to amaze me.)
6. I hate (hypocrisy.)
7. I wish (I could always be happy.)
8. My mother (is divorced from my father.)
9. Men are (human beings.)

10. My life (is what I've made it.)
11. I need (to be happy.)
12. The best
13. When I'm alone (I get lonely.)
14. My work
15. Marriage is (a goal.)
16. My health (is satisfactory.)
17. What annoys me is (hypocrisy.)
18. My father (is a pretty groovy dad.)
19. Sexual relationships (are a natural thing.)
20. My ambition is (to be as happy as I possibly can.)
21. The worst (is yet to come.)
22. Studying (is a drag.)
23. I avoid (getting into arguments and being unhappy.)
24. My nerves (are pretty strong.)
25. I consider myself to be (a very lucky person.)
26. Dirty (water.)
27. I fear (losing my friends.)
28. My mind (is at work all the time.)
29. My home (is somewhat a happy normal one.)
30. I regret (people who feel sorry for themselves.)
31. Most women (are normal.)
32. The future (is what you live for.)
33. As a child, I (was always the one made much of.)
34. What thrills me is (excitement.)
35. Drinking (is a need we all have.)
36. My disposition (is friendly, loving and happy.)
37. Few people know that I (have a secret goal of having quints.)
38. I am proudest of (my achievements.)
39. I get depressed (when I am upset, sick, and unhappy.)
40. I am closest to (Mary Smith.)
41. People consider me (a pretty honest, happy, fun-and-go-lucky type of person with a lot of deep feelings for my friends.)
42. I look forward to (anything that is fun and makes me happy.)
43. I am ashamed of (my faults.)
44. I wish people would (be frank, honest, and trustworthy.)
45. My worst fault is (procrastination.)
46. I feel (happy.)
47. I sometimes think (of what it would be like to be rich.)
48. My biggest worry (is to lose all my friends.)

49. My greatest joy (is to be in love.)
50. Secretly (I want a child.)

Incomplete-Sentence Test
(Form IC-S) for Student Z

Complete these sentences to express how you really feel. Work rapidly and try to be fully frank. Sometimes a word will suffice to complete your idea; sometimes a phrase or a sentence will best convey your thought. Try to reveal as much of your feelings as you can.

1. I like (to play baseball.)
2. At night (I usually stop for a beer.)
3. Children (are okay.)
4. School is (alright.)
5. Other people (interest me.)
6. I hate (to clean the yard.)
7. I wish (I could take a vacation.)
8. My mother (is old.)
9. Men are (people.)
10. My life (is a ball.)
11. I need (to improve on my vocabulary.)
12. The best (thing in life is food.)
13. When I'm alone (it doesn't bother me.)
14. My work (I enjoy.)
15. Marriage is (fine if you're prepared.)
16. My health (could be better.)
17. What annoys me is (loud-mouth people.)
18. My father (works too hard.)
19. Sexual relationships (are wonderful.)
20. My ambition is (to be able to coach a little league team.)
21. The worst (thing in life is to be broke.)
22. Studying (is okay if you are interested.)
23. I avoid (nosey people.)
24. My nerves (always act up once in a while.)
25. I consider myself to be (quiet.)
26. Dirty (is like my car.)
27. I fear (snakes.)
28. My mind (is normal.)
29. My home (is in a small town.)
30. I regret (not firing someone earlier.)
31. Most women (talk too much.)
32. The future (lies ahead.)

33. As a child, I (was very shy.)
34. What thrills me is (watching an exciting basketball game.)
35. Drinking (I do.)
36. My disposition (at work is solid.)
37. Few people know that I (play the trumpet.)
38. I am proudest of (my two boys.)
39. I get depressed (when I receive all the bills.)
40. I am closest to (my wife.)
41. People consider me (mean.)
42. I look forward to (playing baseball and managing.)
43. I am ashamed of (my appearance when not dressed properly.)
44. I wish people would
45. My worst fault is (saying uh and not what.)
46. I feel (tired.)
47. I sometimes think (of being single again.)
48. My biggest worry (is my oldest boy.)
49. My greatest joy (is accomplishing a hard task.)
50. Secretly (once in a while I will sneak out from work.)

STEP 5

Now that you have been over all the items on both tests and scored them, turn to the self-interpretations based on the Incomplete Sentence Test made by the students *Y* and *Z.* Look at your classification chart as you read, and see if you think the interpretations given by each student are justified by the items on his test.

Since these self-interpretations are far from perfect, suggest ways in which you feel that the interpretations could be made more valid in terms of your scoring of the items.

STEP 6

Ask your instructor for the Incomplete Sentence Test which you took earlier in the semester and repeat the same procedure with it which you did for students *Y* and *Z.* Then write your own interpretation of yourself using the results of this test as the basis for what you write.

Self Interpretation
Written by Student Y

What I'm about to say will be for some part hard for me to put down in words my true feelings concerning myself.

As I look at myself trying to find my true identity, I see a person who needs to be happy and loved. This is shown by my answer from "Incomplete Sentence Test," example *7, I wish*—I could always be happy; *11, I need*—to be happy, *20, my ambition is*—to be as happy as I can; *36, My disposition*—is friendly, loving and happy; *46, I feel*—happy. I also find that I place a lot of value on friendship. This is shown by *48, My biggest worry*—is to lose all my friends; *40, I am closest to*—Mary Smith, who is my best friend; *27, I fear*—losing my friends.

I feel I'm a pretty outgoing person who loves other people, life and the result of the combination of the two; *1, I Like*—people.

When it comes to the other side of the coin of happiness, you find sadness. Of course everyone experiences it most of their life, for good comes with the bad. I find that when I'm sad, lonely or feeling as if I'm not loved I get depressed as in *39, I get depressed*—when I'm upset, sad and unhappy.

Truth, honesty, and being frank are what I try to find in others and myself. This is shown in questions *44, I wish people could*—be frank, honest, and trustworthy; *17, What annoys me is*—hypocrisy; *6, I hate*—hypocrisy.

Question 43 reads, *I am ashamed of*—I answered "my faults." Number 45, *My worst fault is*—procrastination. I find myself putting things off until another time and when the time comes, I find another excuse. This, I see now as a typical example of the use of my defenses. I give myself what seems as a very important reason why I can't do it and then when I find out the result which is not good, I have anxiety frustration because of the result. I could keep on having this feeling until I make the right decision, which I find very hard to do. The need of discipline and responsibility is what I need, *22; Studying*—is a drag when you don't like what you are studying, *45*, (in the text).

According to *38, I am proudest of*—my achievements; and 10, *My life*—is what I've made of it, shows me that throughout my life, mostly the last two years, I have molded my life to suit myself of which I am not ashamed. I am not saying it is the best I could have done but as I said, "It's what I've made it", though I at times try to change it when I really feel I should.

My relation with my family is, according to *29, My home is*—somewhat a happy normal one; *8, My mother*—is divorced from my father; *18, My father*—is a pretty cool dad. I find conflicts between the two, since we, my sister and I live with my father. Problems arise and I feel stuck right in the middle with a big conflict of plus plus, which is a very hard one to choose between. I sometimes find some explanation for one side or the other but when I look back on it I feel somewhat guilty. Then there is my sister who I just can't talk to. We can't relate to each other. We are complete opposites. We are always in conflict; this is another problem I have. I am very concerned with her and I can't seem to help her.

After doing this paper I find that the things I have talked about are all very important to me and now when I find myself wondering what is going to come of me I will think of what I have learned in this class and what I wrote in this paper and I will find it much easier to understand.

Self-Interpretation
Written by Student Z

Just from what the Incomplete Sentence Test shows on myself I stated in sentence *16* my health could be better, *24* my nerves always act up once in a while. In *16* this is very true; my health could be improved on since I have a very bad habit of drinking and smoking too much, which does not help my asthma a bit. I know in *24* I pertain this more towards a group of children with constant shouting and crying. In *46*, "I feel tired," this is more of a feeling felt at the time of completing the sentence test. Number *47* states I sometimes think of being single again; this is more or less a thought and how I would change a few of my habits or ways if I did have a chance of becoming single again. These are some of the negative feelings I had. Now I will give a few of the positive feelings on myself. In *13* I stated that when I'm alone it doesn't bother me. This is a feeling where I myself don't feel uncomfortable when alone.

Now in my feelings towards others: I have down in question *23*, I avoid nosey people; *31*, most women talk too much; and *17*, what annoys me is loud-mouth people. Number *31* is a feeling towards women where I work, and not really towards all women outside. In *17* this is more towards people who are intoxicated and start getting violent and loud-mouth. These were some of the negative feelings towards others. Now I will list a few of the positive feelings on others. Number *34*, what thrills me is watching an exciting basketball game; *42*, I look forward to playing baseball and managing; *1*, I like to play baseball; *5*, other people interest me; and *20*, my ambition is to be able to coach a little league team. The reason I categorized these into others was because all the sports mentioned have to do with people who participate. In number 5 I mentioned that other people interest me. This statement is very true and I think this derived from my present position at work.

In the home and family I stated in question *6*, I hate to clean the yard. This negative feeling is true because I do hate to do this because of my hay fever and asthma. Comparing *39* and *47*—in number *39* I get depressed when I receive all the bills, and *47*, I sometimes think of being single again. Number *39* is one of the reasons where *47* derived from. Feelings (positive) towards the family are *40;* I am closest to my wife, and *38,* I am proudest of my two boys.

Under school, *22*, studying is okay if you're interested; and *4*, school is alright; these two statements don't show any real dislike or like for school. The worst thing in life is to be broke—this is one of the negative feelings in the past category which has been experienced by myself. Number *33*—as a child, I was very shy—this could be possibly one of the reasons for dislike for loud-mouth people.

In the future the only thing that seems to be for sure is to be involved with baseball and children.

My job involved with me shows that I enjoy my work (*14*) and that my position is solid. The only negative feeling towards work was *50*—secretly once in a while I will sneak out from work. This statement pertains to the times I sneaked out to be ahead of the quitting time rush.

GAINING INSIGHT THROUGH IMPROMPTU STORIES

The following are a series of stories written without any previous preparation by students in a beginning psychology class. They were asked to write a story of not more than five sentences on each of the indicated subjects.

1. Read these stories carefully.
2. Since a story usually reflects something about the author, what significant needs and pressures do these stories reveal in the lives of these students?
3. Which of these students seems to have the most positive self concept? Why?
4. Do you get any clues as to who the significant others in the lives of these students may be?
5. How do these students feel about life in general? About people? About school? About work?
6. Is there a consistent feeling-tone running through the three stories of each student? What does this tell you about the student?
7. Have any items in the *UK* of these students come through to you in a camouflaged form?
8. What about conflicts and frustrations—are any indicated? If so, is there any indication of the style of adjustment to them?
9. Analyze the three stories you wrote earlier in the light of what you have learned above.

By Student A:

1. A BOY AND A GUN

A small boy liked to play with guns. He played cowboys and indians when he was very small. As he got older, he liked to play army. When he was older he went hunting with his Dad. He didn't like guns so much when he was drafted into the army.

2. A GIRL AND A TEACHER

A girl had a teacher whom she liked very much. She and her girl friends would stay after school to erase blackboards, clean erasers, etc. Once they went to school on a school holiday to help the teacher. They had this teacher for first and second grade. When they were promoted they cried because they had to leave her.

3. A MAN AND HIS BOSS

A man once had a boss who had a bad temper. He was always jumping on his men if they made mistakes or asked questions about the job. The man didn't like the unfairness of his boss. When he was in charge he tried to be firm but fair and the other men seemed to appreciate this.

By Student B:

1. A BOY AND A GUN

Johnny came into the nursery with a water gun. It was the first time I had ever seen him so I proceeded to tell him about all the different things that he could do in the playroom. He didn't seem to be interested until we came to the bathroom with the sink—he ran over to fill his gun with water.

2. A GIRL AND A TEACHER

Mr. Hiclas was her science teacher. Science was not one of her popular subjects, but she was fascinated by Mr. Hiclas, so she was determined to do her best in the class. Whenever he asked questions she was always one of the first to answer.

3. A MAN AND HIS BOSS

Mr. Bell looked at the clock for the second time. Ed was late again and he wondered what excuse he would give this time. When Ed finally came in—20 minutes late—he was all out of breath and said there was a traffic accident.

By Student C:

1. A BOY AND A GUN

A young boy found an old gun in a vacant lot. He knew that guns were dangerous, and yet he started playing with it anyway. His imagination ran wild, and he was soon in a dream world of soldiers and war. The gun accidently went off; and when the boy finally realized what had happened, he ran to his dog and cried.

2. A GIRL AND A TEACHER

Carol did not usually like teachers; however, when she was in high school, she had a teacher who seemed to really understand and appreciate her as a person. This helped her tremendously, and she was gradually able to understand and appreciate teachers as persons.

3. A MAN AND HIS BOSS

A man should not feel inferior to his boss, because they are both human beings. And yet, a man must have respect for authority. A man I know seems very happy with his family and his life and I think it has a lot to do with his feelings of accomplishment in his work.

By Student D:

1. A BOY AND A GUN

Bill had always dreamed of going on safari in Africa. The "Big White Hunter"—that was nine year old Bill Johnson. The only trouble was that Billy didn't have a gun. Well, I take that back; he *did* have a B-B gun. Anyway he's a step closer to making his dream a reality because tin cans aren't that different a target to shoot at than elephants, are they?

2. A GIRL AND A TEACHER

Sue got along fine with her math teacher. She was even teacher's pet! She was the only one the teacher let chew gum in class. Also, she always got A's on her test. And do you know why? The teacher was Sue's father.

3. A MAN AND HIS BOSS

Glen was a good worker. He could move faster than anyone at the plant. It is a wonder that he had so much energy to burn, for no one else did. The people there finally asked him where he got his energy. Glen answered, I eat a Hershey bar an hour before work each day.

By Student E:

1. A BOY AND A GUN

Johnny was very proud. At the age of nine he owned his own, real rifle. His father bought him a target to shoot at, but Johnny didn't like it. Johnny liked to shoot doves and pigeons and squirrels and rabbits. Ten years went by until Johnny learned not to like guns because now he had to carry one.

2. A GIRL AND A TEACHER

Susan hated school and books but she especially hated teachers. She especially hated one particular teacher. The teacher was an old woman who tried to make Susan learn boring things. This teacher was grouchy and mean and old and ugly. One day the teacher told Susan that she was very smart and would have to move up a grade and from then on that old teacher was Susan's favorite.

3. A MAN AND HIS BOSS

Mr. Jones was a good worker and a good man. Everything Mr. Jones's boss would tell him to do he would do. "A business needs discipline," Mr. Jones would say, and what he preached he practiced. The business went bankrupt and the boss left the country. Mr. Jones was quite upset.

By Student F:

1. A BOY AND A GUN

Walking through the high grass, the wind blowing in his face, the boy noticed something moving in a peculiar manner off to his left. He raised his rifle to shoot. He squeezed off one shot and walked towards his prey. When he arrived his father was lying on the ground, dead.

2. A GIRL AND A TEACHER

She had been sitting in the front of his class for almost a year. The young man who was the teacher couldn't help but tell himself that he was in love.

He had only one hang-up and that was his wife. The young man became quite frustrated, so one day he quietly disposed of his hang-up.

3. A MAN AND HIS BOSS

"You're not doing a good job," the foreman told him. It was a very large steel mill and there was a lot of work to be done. The elderly man knew he was holding his share of work.

One day the foreman was checking one of the big pots of molten steel; the old man reminiscing with a smile on his face, still could not understand till this day how the foreman fell in.

SEEING YOURSELF IN PERSPECTIVE

Bring a mirror to class large enough to see your face. Your teacher will show you how you are to use it when you come to class.

CONCLUSION: DESCRIBING YOUR SELF

Now that you have explored your self through the four ways described above, use all these four sets of materials to write a complete description of what you are, how you came to be, and what makes you "tick." This should be your masterpiece. If it does not please you, you might explain at the end your feelings about this description of you. Can you suggest ways in which this description of you could be improved?

4

RELATIONSHIPS FROM YOUR ROOTS

INTRODUCTION

In the last chapter you investigated, told about, and looked at your self. You then used all these experiences and data to paint as complete a picture of yourself as you could. This is your inner self. It is the part of you which is most intimate *within* you. Before this experience, parts of your self were hidden—perhaps even from you. You have now begun to reveal what your self really is. This will help you to know where you really are at.

But, of course, you are more than just this inner self. In your autobiography, and your various other looks at your self, you saw and told very little of where you came from, what you identified with in your background, how you relate to, and feel about, your family. These origins and ties are your roots, and like a plant, you are nourished by a network of roots. Many of these roots may seem to hold you back and restrict your growth and freedom. Many of them may be unknown to you. Many of them may be of no concern to you—you "couldn't care less." However, without these roots, you wouldn't *be* at all—nor could you grow or have come into being.

It is the purpose of this chapter to help you understand this part of your outer self—and particularly to understand your feelings about these roots. In addition, its purpose is to help you use these roots as a means of strength and support rather than as a means for limitation and restriction.

WHAT ARE ROOTS?

Now let's talk about roots a bit. Where are they? What are they? Are roots just people, such as parents, grandparents, uncles, aunts, cousins, and so on? Or are there other kinds of roots? Yes, roots certainly are people, or groups of people, in the sense we are using them here. We may feel rooted to a place, a house, or an object, but usually it is the social context—the people associated with this object—which makes you feel rooted to it. Therefore, roots are not just individual persons, but groups of persons as well. They may be the members of your family who produced you biologically, such as your parents, grandparents, and great-grandparents. And they may be those who come along with these biological roots and hopefully give you support, such as your brothers, sisters, uncles, aunts, and cousins. But you also may have roots in institutions, organizations, or less formalized groups of people. These groups might be composed of people of similar religious beliefs; people who came from the same foreign country; residents of the same city, state, locality, or neighborhood; members of the same race; members of an organization—social, fraternal, or political, people who earn, or intend to earn, their living in a particular profession, trade, or enterprise; or people who enjoy or participate in similar sports, hobbies, or other kinds of fun. For example, Roberto Chavez, who lives in Azusa in the San Gabriel Valley of Southern California, identifies himself as a Chicano. He is a member of United Mexican American Students (UMAS); he is a Catholic; he is a member of his school's basketball team and regularly goes with a group of his friends to rock concerts. He is studying engineering. His organizational or institutional roots would probably consist of (1) his identification with Azusa, San Gabriel Valley, California; (2) his ethnic identity—Chicano; (3) his religious identity—Catholic; (4) his organizational membership—UMAS; (5) his "fun roots"—basketball team and rock concert buddies; and (6) his future profession in engineering.

George Williams, who lives in Los Angeles, identifies himself as a white American. He belongs to the Baptist Church; he is a member of the school's swimming team; he is a pre-med student; he has joined Kappa Kappa Kappa fraternity and enjoys surfing and skiing very much. He belongs to a skiing club, but usually surfs by himself or with a few of his friends. Can you pick out George's organizational and institutional roots? Remember, it is the individual's *feeling of involvement* which determines whether the root is actually there and functioning—not just his "paper" membership, street address, or registration in a course of study.

These are some of the kinds of roots which you *may* have. Those of us who talk about our roots seem to feel that we are connected to or supported by, one or more of these kinds of roots. In some cases, we are rooted to individuals or groups which are no longer alive—such as a parent or grandparent who is now dead, or a group, organization, or team to which we belonged in years past which no longer exists today. Nevertheless, such roots may be strong psychological forces in our lives today.

But what about those who say, "I couldn't care less. I know

nothing, or very little, about my family, and what I do know I would like to forget and be free of"? And what about others who say, "I belong to no groups. I identify with no groups. I feel best when I am alone out in the open, or when I am doing my thing by myself. It is groups and institutions that have hung me up. And it is my ties with the institutions of this Establishment—which you say were built by my so-called roots—which I need to split from"? Of course, these are very honest reactions and carry with them very deep, intense, and important feelings. Therefore, they need to be examined very carefully. Dead roots—roots that are psychologically dead, that is—need to be pulled up and discarded. Live roots need to be discovered, tested, watered, and nourished so that they can in turn support you. Roots make trouble usually *when we don't know* (1) whether we are connected to them or not; (2) whether they are dead or alive psychologically; and (3) how much stress they can take. For these reasons, knowledge of roots is a help in developing personal security and reducing fear about the future and the sources of support upon which you can count.

UNCOVERING ROOTS

Let us now discover how we can uncover our roots—scrape back the "earth" of the surrounding culture—and lay them bare for our examination and conscious evaluation. Later on we will want to proceed to the extremely difficult task of revealing our feelings about these roots and perhaps testing their relative strength and ability to give us sustenance.

For this purpose, let us listen to how Joan Baez, a contemporary singer whom you've probably heard, talk about her roots in her autobiography, *Daybreak.*

My Mother

Mother was born in Scotland, and brought to America when she was two. Her mother died when she was three. Her father was a very far-out Episcopalian minister who loved the theater, sang off-key from the pulpit, dressed his children out of the missionary barrel, fought a firey public battle with the DAR, and had a weakness for marrying domineering women. Mother says I would have loved him. I can think of only one picture of him. A portrait showing a weak, thin-nosed, rather nice-looking sad man. There comes to mind now a picture of Mother's mother, carrying Mother's sisters on her back! She is very pretty, also sad, tilting her head back as though to bump it in a nice way against the baby's head. Now I think of the picture of mother which I have hanging in my house. It was taken when she was ten. She is standing on a beach in the wind with the ocean in back of her, her arms outstretched in youthful grace, her dark legs poking out of an oversized bathing costume coming a bit together at the knees, the wind blowing her hair across her face, across an exquisite smile. Her head is tilted back as though butting the wind. She is like a lovely bit of dark heather. She has kept the grace and beauty through unbelievable odds. Odds which have given her a power and wisdom which she tries very hard not to acknowledge.

Her first stepmother was classically frigid, and appears dressed in white, smiling very sweetly, in all the old albums. She's the one who would hand mother and her sister fifteen cents and say, "Here's your allowance for this week," and before they could close their fingers over the coins, she'd say, "and now, because you've spilled the ink in the study and made a mess in the john and stolen peanut butter from the big jar, I am taking it away. Maybe you can learn to be good children, and then you will get your allowance." Money was dirty to touch, Jews were dirty to live near, sex was dirty to think about or have; children were taught by punishment; and in the meantime dressing everyone in white frocks would tide things over . . .

The next stepmother, (Meg), was a six-foot-tall redhead schizophrenic who made puppets and dressed in purple and orange and was prone to chasing Mother's father around the house waving a butcher knife and screaming . . .

Meg's sadistic energies were centered on (Mother's) older sister, because of her closeness to her father, and Mother was more often than not just ignored.

(Mother) declared her independence when she was thirteen. Meg threw a pot of steaming boiled potatoes at her from across the room. Mother ducked and went about washing the dishes. Meg came up behind her and slapped her full strength on the side of the face. Mother whirled around and said, "Damn you!" and Meg froze in shock. When she regained her fury she raised her arms to beat Mother, but Mother caught her arms mid-flight with her own slippery hands and lowered them to her sides, saying, "Don't you ever do that again." Meg fumbled in her defeat, and finally said, "Go outside and fill this up with berries," handing Mother a pot, and Mother said, "If you want berries, pick them yourself." From then on Mother kept her coat hanging near the front door, with two nickles in the pocket, one for bus fare, and the other to call a friend.

At some point in her childhood she lived in a sort of gypsy

camp for a while, eating potato crusts charcoaled in the fire on sticks. She and her little friends ate them because there wasn't much food around and no one bothered to feed the children. She found communion wafers delightful, but not very filling. And she was guilty of stealing peanut butter—she would steal it in great globs, knowing that she would eventually be caught and punished. She's not hungry like that anymore, but she still has a craving for peanut butter . . .

In a snapshot taken of her when she was about eighteen she stands sideways to the camera, dressed in satin, with some feathery shawl around her shoulders, her eyes looking into the lens. She is a vamp, a gypsy queen, a mystic, a blueblood. She is all of those things still, and the battle rages inside and outside Mother as to whether she will ever admit to the fact that she is glorious.

My Father

My father is short, honest, dark, and very handsome. He's good, he's a good man. He was born in Mexico, and brought up in Brooklyn. His father was a Mexican who left the Catholic church to become a Methodist minister. My father worked hard in school. He loved God and the church and his parents. At one time in his life he was going to be a minister, but the hypocrisy of the church bothered him and he became a scientist instead. He has a vision of how science can play the major role in saving the world. This vision puts a light into his eyes. He is a compulsive worker, and I know that he will never stop his work long enough to have a look at some of the things in his life which are blind and tragic. But it's not my business to print. About me and my father I don't know. I keep thinking of how hard it was for him to say anything nice about me to my face. Maybe he favored me and felt guilty about it, but he couldn't say anything nice. A lot of time I thought he would break my heart. Once he complimented me for something I was wearing. "You ought to wear that kind of thing more often," he said, and I looked into the mirror and I was wearing a black dress which I hated. I was fourteen then and I remember thinking, "Hah. I remind him of his mother in this thing."

My father is the saint of the family. You work at something until you exhaust yourself, so that you can be good at it, and with it you try to improve the lot of the sad ones, the hungry ones, the sick ones. You raise your children trying to teach them decency and a respect for human life. Once when I was thirteen he asked me if I would accept a large sum of money for the death of a man who was going to die anyway. I didn't quite understand. If I was off the hook, and just standing by, and then the man was killed by someone else, why shouldn't I take a couple of million? I told him sure, I'd take the money, and he laughed his head off. "That's immoral," he said. I didn't know what immoral meant, but I knew something was definitely wrong taking money for a man's life . . .

My father teaches physics. He is a Ph.D. in physics, and we all wish he'd had just one boy who wasn't so opposed to school, to degrees, to formal education of any kind. One child to show some interest when he does physics experiments at the dinner table. But then it must be partly because we felt obligated to be student-types that we have rebelled so completely. I can barely read. That is to say, I would rather do a thousand things before sitting down to read.

He used to tell us we should read the dictionary. He said it was fun and very educational. I've never gotten to it . . .

Next thing I knew we were packing up and moving across the country. My father had taken a job as a professor of physics at the University of Redlands for about one-half the pay, and one-tenth the prestige—against the advice of everyone he knew except my mother. Since leaving Buffalo in 1947, he's never accepted a job that has anything to do with armaments, offense, defense, or whatever they prefer to call it. . . .

I don't think he's ever understood me very well. He's never understood my compulsiveness, my brashness, my neurosis, my fears, my antinationalism (though he's changing on that), my sex habits, my loose way of handling money. I think often I startle him, and many times I please him. . . .

My father wrote that it always amazed him how I came to conclusions intuitively which took him years to realize.

Notice that Joan does not describe completely all of her roots in the excerpt from her autobiography. She does not even do a complete job in the whole book. However, it will be helpful to lay bare what she does describe. When you follow this process with yourself, you will find that in "laying bare," other previously unknown roots may come to light. For this purpose let us use the diagrams in Figures 4-1 and 4-2.

Figure 4-1a shows you with many roots and root branches tied to you or feeding into you, depending on how you look at it. From the labels you can see that those individual branches correspond to individual members of your family constellation. When you make your family roots diagram, you may find that you do not have family members who correspond to each of the branches in Figure 4-1a, such as step-parents, uncles, aunts and cousins. Furthermore, you may have to add additional branches if you have more sisters or brothers or members of any other family category than are provided in our dia-

FIG. 4–1a. **YOUR FAMILY ROOTS**

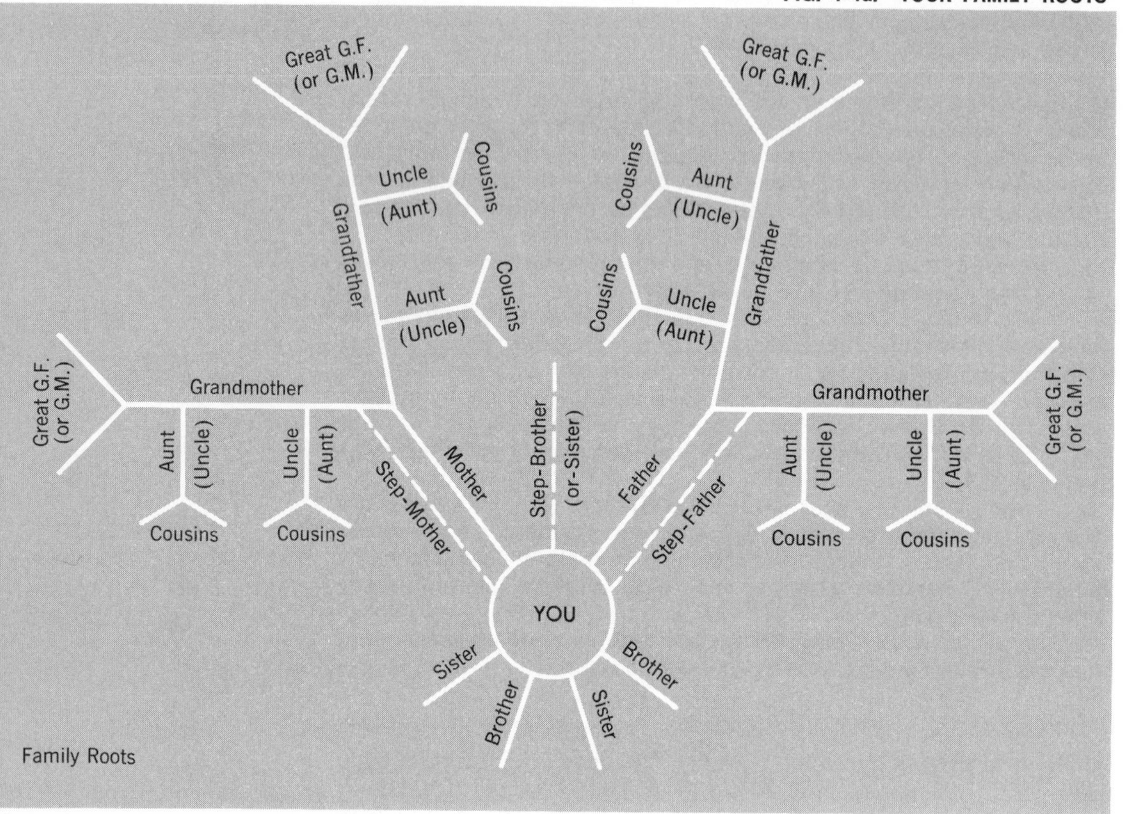

grams. In order to see how this diagram works, let us see how it would be filled in from the data Joan gives us. This diagram is Figure 4-1b.

We find that Joan has a father and mother, two grandfathers, and on her mother's side two step-grandmothers. Her father's mother is not mentioned except to say that her father loved his parents. Her mother's real mother is barely mentioned also. Joan has an aunt, her mother's sister, and she refers to other children as "us," but does not say here how many there are or what sex. (Actually she has two sisters, Pauline and Mimi). Again, when you do this for yourself, you will have on hand much more data than we have for Joan, and you can question other members of your family and get even more data.

FIG. 4–1b. FAMILY ROOTS FOR JOAN BAEZ

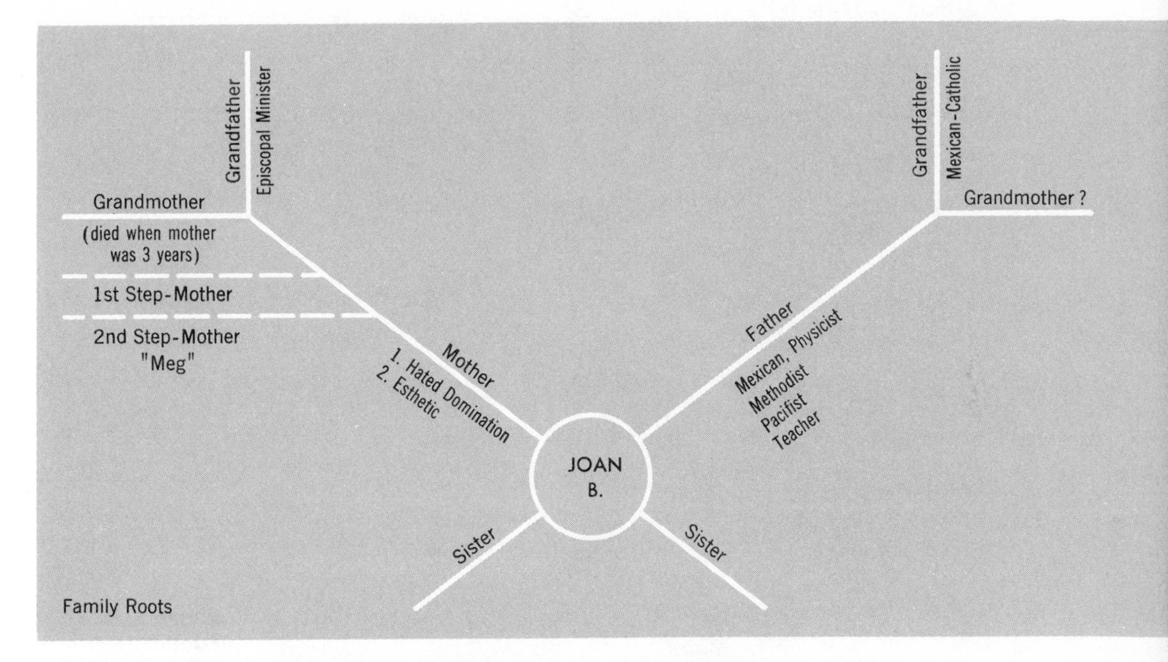

You should in any case fill in the diagram for you as fully as you can.

Now let us look at Figure 4-2a. This diagram shows you surrounded by all your group and organizational roots. Those which are filled in are just suggestive; when you make a diagram, you will need to include *all* of the roots of this kind you can think of—whether you like them or not. Now look at Figure 4-2b. This is how Joan's roots would look.

First there are the national roots—Scotch on her mother's side and Mexican on her father's side; then the religious roots—strong Episcopalian from grandfather, Catholic, turned Methodist, from her father. Father contributes a respect for science and formal education. Mother seems less formal, more humanistic and "outdoors oriented." Father identifies with nationality and ethical justice for all. Mother identifies with individual persons and tends to sacrifice reason for sensitivity towards others. Both parents accept and associate with a wide diversity of types of persons. Father would perhaps want to understand and help them. Mother would love them. Joan's iden-

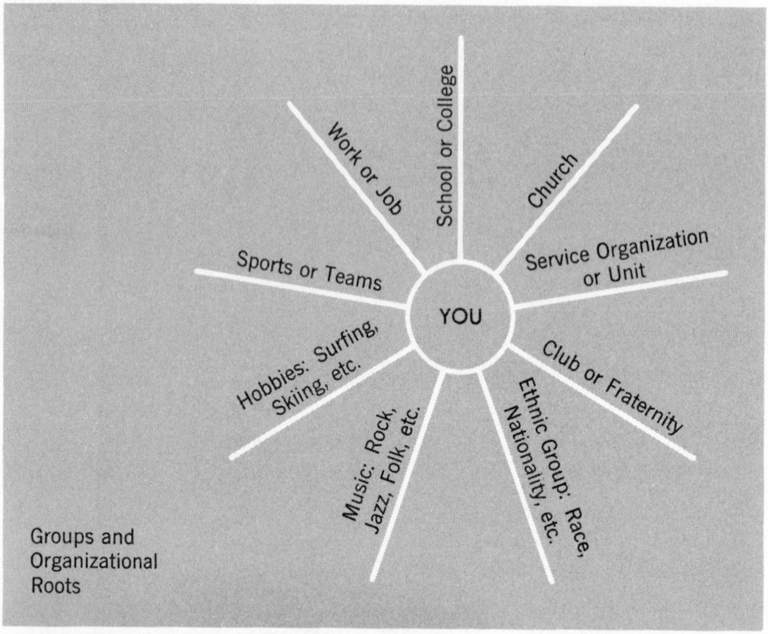

School or College
Work or Job
Church
Sports or Teams
Service Organization or Unit
YOU
Hobbies: Surfing, Skiing, etc.
Club or Fraternity
Music: Rock, Jazz, Folk, etc.
Ethnic Group: Race, Nationality, etc.
Groups and Organizational Roots

FIG. 4–2a. YOUR GROUPS AND ORGANIZATIONAL ROOTS

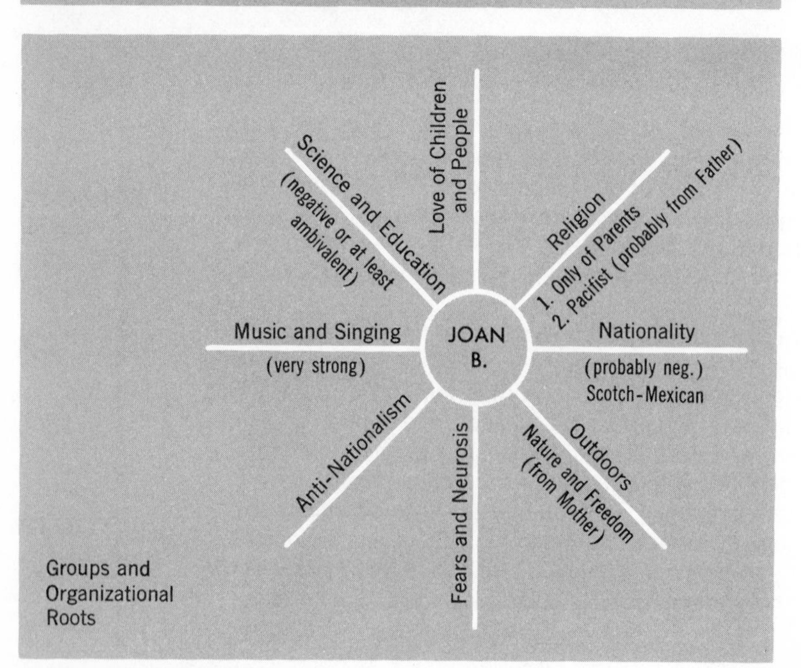

FIG. 4–2b. GROUPS AND ORGANIZATIONAL ROOTS FOR JOAN BAEZ

tifications are a complex of these as can be seen from her descriptions of father and mother.

Figure 4-3 gives us a third kind of roots diagram in chronological perspective. We have no idea of this kind for Joan here (although the data are in her complete autobiography.) However, you will be able to fill in this kind of a diagram quite well for you. You will again have to make your own diagram indicating at the three age levels who are the persons who are particularly "rooted" to you. If there are organizational roots at any of these levels—such as Boy or Girl Scouts, and so on—include them, too.

It may help you if you use the following questionnaire to collect the data for your three diagrams.

Family Roots

1. Your full name ________________ Age ____
2. Father's name ________________ Sisters and Brothers
   Mother's name ________________ ________________
   ____
3. Grandparents:
   Mother's ________________ ________________
   Father's ________________ ________________
4. Uncles and Aunts (give whether from Mother's or Father's family.)
5. Cousins (give whether from Mother's or Father's family)
6. Other family roots.
7. What interesting stories do you know about any of these people? ________________

Group and Organizational Roots

1. Sex ________________ 2. Race ________________
3. Residence ________________
4. Nationality ________________
   Nationality of Mother ________________
   Nationality of Father ________________

FIG. 4–3. SIGNIFICANT PERSONS AT DIFFERENT TIMES IN YOUR LIFE

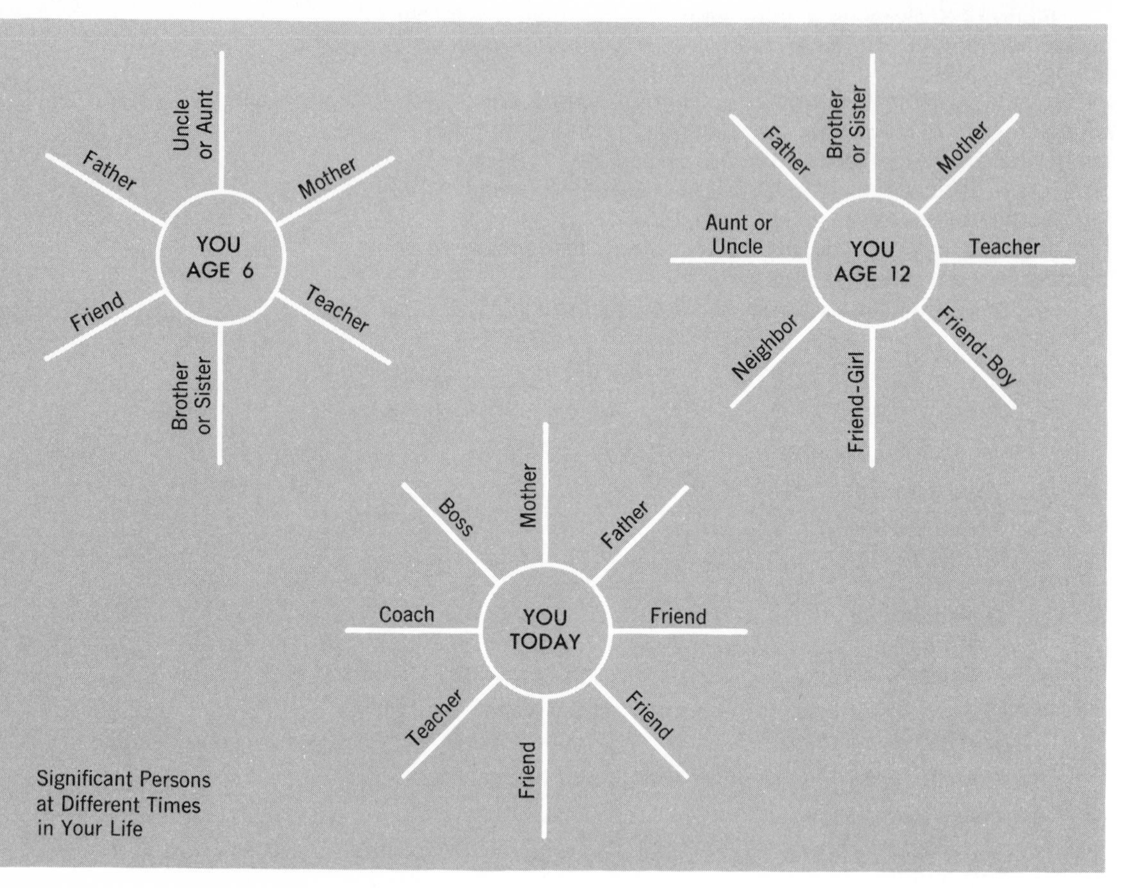

5. Religion ______________________

6. Groups and Organizations you belong to or identify with

____

____

7. Which of all the above groups and organizations do you feel closest to (list the first three in order of your preference)

   1. ______________________
   2. ______________________
   3. ______________________

AGE 6

1. Who were members of your family at this age?
2. What close friends did you have?
3. What groups—other than your family—were you associated with?

AGE 12

1. Who were the members of your family at this age?
2. What close friends did you have?
3. What groups—other than your family—were you associated with?

PRESENT

1. Who are the members of your family at this time?
2. What close friends do you have?
3. What groups—other than your family—are you associated with?

When you have finished all these diagrams for yourself, you will have laid your roots bare. You must now investigate your feelings about these roots, but first you will learn a bit about feelings, dreams, and how they operate with respect to roots.

FEELINGS, DREAMS, AND ROOTS

A root—one of *your* roots, for instance—may be alive, or it may be dead. It may be an asset to your life, or it may be a drag. This is no news. We have all cut ourselves off from parts of our past, and we have felt the restricting pull of family demands in the present. What is less often understood is that your conscious evaluation of a particular root may be in error. You may consider—or act as though you considered—a root alive, and yet it may be only a ghost of what it was. This phenomenon is quite familiar to those of us who have gone away to college or into the service—thinking very positively about our friends back home, but finding when we return that our ties to those people are dead and lifeless. We wonder how we could ever have had such ties. Furthermore, ties to family which are painfully restrictive during school years may become an asset and a source of support after marriage or leaving home. We wonder how we could ever have objected to them, and we see them, in retrospect, as quite positive.

These are examples of the fact that our *feelings* about things—particularly things which are close to us, like our roots—are often not authentic. We fool ourselves and try to make the feelings what we think they ought to be, or what we want them to be—rather than what they are. In so doing we split ourselves into a good and a bad, a right and a wrong, a self which we want to be, and a self which we are. See the section on exploring and releasing your feelings. p. 118 in Chapter 5 for ways of dealing with this condition.

Now how does this rather confusing situation come about? You were not born with unauthentic expressions of feelings. When, as an infant, you were cold or hungry, you cried; when you were well-fed and content, you slept and were at peace. However, very early you learned that to express certain kinds of feelings—such as rage or resentment—was not acceptable, and if you persisted in expressing them you would be punished bodily or by being excluded from the family company.

As you grew up towards maturity, you found that certain feelings—such as the sex drive, for instance, could rarely be expressed at all, except in private. Other feelings—such as extreme resentment—were limited to the athletic field or the dramatic stage, but rarely were tolerated in day-to-day affairs. You learned that feelings of attraction or rejection towards another person—or even towards some possession of his, such as an article of clothing, or a feature of his face or body—must be carefully controlled and if expressed at all, must be cautiously reduced in intensity, camouflaged, or even reversed. For instance, it is well understood that I may not acceptably start a fight with you in "polite society." But it is also disastrous for me to express my full admiration of your wife's or girl friend's physical appearance, or my revulsion at the lack of esthetic design of your new house, or how much I dislike your new car. As a result of these social demands, our feelings become suppressed—to the extent that we do not know, with certainty, what they *are*. We only know what they ought to be, and if the suppressed feeling is strong enough, we may not be able to express *any* feeling at all—for fear that the wrong one will be expressed. This fear leads some persons to make responses on the incomplete sentence test such as "My mother is a wonderful woman" and "I look forward to when I can leave home and be free of my mother's nagging"–both responses coming from the same person. Such a person is really saying, "I feel really quite negative towards these roots which come from my mother—but I know that is not acceptable because everyone should love and respect his mother—*but I don't*." If these feelings are *both* strong enough, this person may leave the item blank. Most blanks on the incomplete sentence test are due to conflicting feelings—not to a "blank mind," which is the reason usually given.

Now if this is the case, how can we ever know our real feelings about our roots and learn how to use them to enrich our life? Fortunately, modern psychology has rediscovered an excellent tool for this purpose—one which has been known for thousands of years and which is familiar to us all: the dream.

If we are to use dreams effectively to understand our feelings about things, there are several ideas about dreams which you must accept—or at least explore.

1. Your dream is you. It is you just as surely as your waking life is you. You don't *have* your dreams, you *are* your dreams—in part. And when you are asleep you *are* your dream completely. This means that the dream came from you. You made it. And the *it* that you made is *you*. Your dream didn't come from somewhere or from somebody else.

   Now this may be hard for you—particularly if you are used to thinking of dreams as carrying strange and occult messages from strange and occult sources; however, if this has been your idea of dream, why don't you *try out* the idea that your dream is you and see what it can do to clarify your feelings about things?

2. Since your dream is you, every part of the dream is you—in one of your aspects. In waking life your face is you. Similarly, in your dream, every part, event, and object is you, because it is something which you made and chose. They are each you in one of your aspects.

3. In your dream, you are to a large extent free of the social restrictions which inhibit the free expression of feelings. Feelings are much more freely expressed—and expressed more authentically—even though the targets for these feelings may be disguised in a symbolic way.
4. It is more helpful to relive your dream than to try to understand, interpret, or explain it. Of course dreams do have meaning, but to focus on the interpretation of the dream is to make an object of it apart from you. And this focus blocks a full expression of the feelings and a clear perception of how those feelings are directed.

"But," you may say, "I don't dream; at least I haven't dreamed for a long time—not since I was a child. I guess this part just doesn't apply to me!"

Wait a minute! Not so fast! Do you *want* to dream? If so here is the way to catch a dream.

Dreams are like fish. They swim in the quiet pools of your self. To catch them you must not be in a hurry. You must be relaxed—a bit excited about your catch, perhaps—but at ease and attentive to your body.

When you are ready to catch a dream—usually this will be when you are ready to go to bed at night—free yourself from your worries by taking a leisurely warm bath. Then, as you lie in your bed at full length, think of people, places, ideas, which interest you. Let your mind go freely—into fantasy if this seems natural—and fill in as many details as you can. As you do this, let your body relax more and more fully. Soon you will be asleep. If you are lucky, this will "put a dream on your hook." But how to land it? As you wake, be as gradual as you can. Often when you awake there is a dream on the hook. So don't bound out of bed. Lie there and attempt to gently reel in your line—that is, run over in your mind the details of the dream. When they seem clear, go directly to your pencil and notebook, which you should keep near your pillow, and write your dream in intimate detail. Another way would be to tell your dream to a tape recorder. Now you have it! If this procedure doesn't produce a dream, repeat the process for several nights consecutively until you are successful. By this means most of us can learn to catch a dream.

With all of the above points in mind and with a willingness to try them out, let us look at a dream of Joan Baez as told in her autobiography.

Dream

Dreamed we all went to work for some evil man. He ran a super-James Bond efficient resort-like science grounds, where he smuggled very expensive stuff and used the hell out of people. Popsy thought it was an advanced science study center, so the family moved there. The director had rules like the ones in the prison. I was playing with a little girl, and we were running on the grass. I saw that they were paving over the grass with oil and gravel, and I was disappointed, because the grass was so pretty. When the child's mother arrived (she was a new employee), I told her the child would get all sticky from the tar, and just then a lady guard approached and said something like "silence rules" which meant that the lady had to act as if she didn't see me. Couldn't speak to me or recognize me. She didn't take it too seriously, so I knew she wouldn't last long there. . . . At one point I was eating a piece of cake, taking the crumbly part out of the frosting and throwing the frosting away, and leaning over a waste basket, and another lady employee stopped typing and checked up on me with obvious disapproval, and I know she was making a note of my bad behavior. . . . There were famous scientists from all over the world, and Popsy was just beginning to settle down and find out his job (he'd been conned into thinking it was wonderful international science work), and Mother and I went off to see a calf get born. The mother cow charged at us, but didn't hurt us. There were always spies in the disguise of scientists wherever we went.

This dream is rather simple but contains many feelings and they are expressed towards many targets. After you have read the dream over again, try to go through it as though you were Joan; see what feelings you have as you do this, and how these feelings change. Now answer the following questions about Joan:

According to Joan's dream

1. What feelings does she have about science?
2. What feelings does she have towards her mother?

3. What feelings does she have towards her father?
4. Which parent does she seem closest to? Which of these roots seems strongest? Most nourishing?
5. What reactions does Joan show towards the Establishment?
6. How does the cake part of the dream make you feel?
7. From this dream, what could you say about Joan's feelings about her roots?
8. Does the dream bring out any feelings which are not in Joan's description of her roots?

Now look at your diagrams and consider your feelings about your roots. Indicate on all three diagrams those roots to which you are (or were) positive by underlining them in red. Indicate those roots to which you are negative by underlining them in blue.

Next: Catch a dream, and write it down carefully, just the way you dreamed it. If you can catch more than one dream, so much the better.

1. Read your dream carefully.
2. Go over the dream, letting yourself *feel* what you naturally feel at each step of the dream.
3. Remembering what we did with Joan's dream, what does your dream tell you about your roots and your feelings towards them?
4. Does the dream tell you anything which the diagrams do not? Do any of the colors—red or blue—change in the dream?

It will help you if you will tell your dream in class and let the class members and your instructor identify feelings which you seem to be having as you relive the dream.

WHAT PLACE DO ROOTS HAVE IN OUR LIVES?

You have now investigated your roots and also some of your feelings about them. You know how you have been nourished and sustained in the past. You know, too, what you are tied to at present. The final step is to trim and redesign your root structure. You, of course, couldn't do this until you *knew* what that structure was. Now you will want to encourage certain roots to grow longer and stronger, and you may want to cut other roots off. You might even want to graft on some new variety of root—although this is a rather difficult process.

But how does one do this? The simplest way is to answer the question "Who are you?" Of course, you could simply answer with your name: Marilyn Moore or Stephen Schwartz. But is this who you are? Or you might give your social security number. Or you might say you are Harry Moore's daughter or Sam Schwartz's son, or the great-grandson of Frederick Douglass. Is *this* who you are? Another way of answering the question "who are you?" is to say, "I am an American, or a German, or a Cambodian, or a Portuguese." You might say, "I am a Baptist, or a Jew, or a Catholic, or a Buddhist." You might say, "I am a carpenter, or a banker, or a teacher, or a truck driver." You might say, "I am a pre-med student, or a psychology major, or an accounting major, or a student nurse." You might say, "I am a Viet Nam veteran, or a football player, or a father of three, or an alcoholic, or a Texan, or a New Yorker, or a rock freak." All these responses are only samples. Some of you might use a long series of descriptions to say who you are. Others might prefer to say only, "I am a human being," or "I am a world citizen," or "I am a man." In other words, some of you might prefer to get your nourishment and support from one, or a few, strong roots. Others might prefer the diverse support and nourishment of many roots—large and small.

Whichever way you choose to do the job of designing and reshaping your roots is your own choice. No one can tell you from what you shall gain your strength. And no one can tell you from what you shall refuse to get your strength either!

DESCRIBING YOUR RELATIONSHIP TO YOUR ROOTS

What follows is the attempt of Kathy, a student, to describe her roots. Since she does so in great detail, it should be easy for you to see her identifications and also to get an idea of how she might answer the question, "Who are you?" even though she does not come right out and do it.

Read her story carefully and try to get the full impact of what she is saying.

"My Roots," by Kathy

My father's family came originally from England and Scotland. The McPhails have their geneology traced back to the first settlers in America. I have the complete history, which came from some organization in Washington, D.C., and it makes interesting reading—the names are so quaint—and I noticed that most of the families included from 2 to 5 children; their occupations include teachers, doctors, lawyers, cabinet-makers, coppersmiths, and farmers.

My father's family was very small; he had one sister with whom I was never too well acquainted. Neither did I visit this Grandma—though she lived within traveling distance; she died, however, when I was very young—perhaps before I was old enough to "go visit overnite" or for a week. This side of my family always had a McPhail reunion every summer at some nearby part—and there I met great aunts and uncles and cousins, "thrice removed"! I liked these people—they seemed very intelligent, dignified folks—gracious and well-spoken.

My father worked in a grocery store—he ran it with another man, for the elderly owner who lived in our town. He worked 6 days a week, year round. Home from lunch at 12:00—and supper at 6:00. He belonged to the Masonic Lodge and was once their Grand Master; one of my most distinct memories of him is the picture of him walking through the house with a little navy blue, leather-covered book in his hand, memorizing something. He also needed a clean white shirt for Lodge night and for the times they were served dinner by the ladies of the Eastern Star—to which my mother did not belong. (Most all Masonic wives do.) He always served on the election boards, and held the office of village assessor for many years. Everyone knew him, and I believe he was loved by his friends and respected by many others; when we drove past our town hall, on the way to the cemetery, I was touched and proud to see the flag at half mast. But I was always proud to be a McPhail. (There were my 3 sisters and my brother, who was the eldest.) And this, in spite of the fact that my father drank too much, and I knew it—and everyone else in town knew it. My mother said he was his own worst enemy. He died at 54—because of it—leaving his family mostly grown; my baby sister was in her last year of high school—but leaving my mother to live (up to now) 31 years as a widow.

My father was a man's man, so I've been told, and I know he enjoyed baseball, hockey, football—any sport. He went deer hunting every fall—but I'll bet that was more for the "male vacation" than for love of shooting deer. He read avidly, a part of every day's routine. He had a good mind, leaving high school a month before graduation to join the naval fleet which Teddy Roosevelt sent round the world (to impress Japan, among others). I have read his letters home to his mother and they are finely written—both in content and penmanship. When he returned from his 4 years of navy life he married my mother who was clerking in his Dad's grocery store in Peoria, Illinois. He was 25; she 23. Why they were ever attracted to one another is beyond me. I don't think my mother knew what being married *was* and my Dad was completely fooled by her looks. Or something! For she is still like a naive child, puritanical in nature—who regards sex as a necessary evil—and you *don't* talk about it. I caught this attitude early, and when I became really curious obtained my information from friends and my eldest sister, (still my best loved friend).

From 12 years on (at least) I have been actively disagreeing with my mother. It has caused me much pain and feelings of great guilt to this day. When we moved to Oregon—away from my family—I am sure the move was made easier for me because it would remove me from this ever-present contention. I *understood* why she held such views. She had to leave school in the 4th or 6th grade—her German family (10 children) and a widowed mother had to eat—and *everyone* worked. Her 3 brothers never married, (4 children died), and the 3 girls did marry. But Grandma Schaffer was a true matriarch and those boys never had a chance! I loved and respected all of them—spending summer vacations with these aunts and uncles, grandma and cousins—sharing holidays always in their company, but having to tolerate their terrible prejudice, their lack of intelligence, their narrowness.

I knew I was not the kind of person my mother was—nor ever could be. I had read too much, and my views already encompassed a world my mother hadn't ever known—nor did she want any part of such a world. I am sure she felt terribly insecure with her lack of education. For she took no part in P.T.A.—nor came to any school functions. She and my Dad had no mutual friends; we had only relatives in our home to visit. At that time, I knew no different, so I was not unhappy about such a way of living. It did not prepare me well, however, to be comfortable with "outsiders." I was painfully shy when I first married, and it was hard to meet my husband's family and their friends.

I never heard my parents fight or argue—he kissed her cheek or the back of her neck, as she went about her work in the kitchen. (I gave them both a kiss on the cheek every nite as I went upstairs to bed.)

My mother's life was made interesting and beautiful through her flower garden. I was always first child up in our house and so perhaps it was natural that it was I who had to "come see what came out in the night." She pumped pails and pails of water and carried them to nourish these plants, and I helped her sometimes. I, too, loved that garden—and I could draw a map picture of it, placing each kind of plant in its exact location! I am sure my love of nature must have come from her, and there are many things—such as family holiday traditions, which she instilled in me—that leave me grateful and even more guilty, as I want not only to be able to agree with her, I want her to be proud of me as I *am*, not as the way she may think I am—or trusts I am. But this is not realistic—and I need to remember this. For in spite of all this, I was secure and happy as a child, and we were taught a deep respect for each other and all adults that has lasted a lifetime.

My sweet little mother has tenacity and spunk and *energy* that would put women 40 years her junior to shame! She has never interfered in her children's lives—nor consented to live with any of them—giving all her energy and time to raising them, yet letting each one go readily when the time came.

But I still come back full circle—to feeling sorry for my Dad, and wishing that his problems might have been solvable so that he might be among us today getting to know my children—and they him. (The McPhails live to be 80–90–100 years old—but not my Dad). I wish he were here for all our sakes, not to mention his. For I think grandparents are vitally important. A child needs to know who he is—what his roots are—to hear stories of the "olden days"' and have a sense of the past so he can know his place in the present and look forward to the future.

Now that you have read Kathy's story, what is it that she is really telling you about herself? In order to answer this, write a paragraph answering the question "Who are you?" as you feel Kathy would do it. Also, do you remember Joe, Randy, Sylvia and Janie in Chapter 1? How do you think they would describe their roots? In their opening statement, they are really answering the question, "Who are you?" As a concluding exercise write your own paragraph answering the question, "Who are you?"

After you have completed all these experiences, now what is your reaction to your roots and their place in your life? Remember this is no place to hide—let all your feelings come out as fully as possible.

RELATIONSHIPS TO AUTHORITY

5

INTRODUCTION

For the last three chapters you have been thinking and talking about things and people in your life who are close to you—your self, your peers, your roots. There are other factors in your life, however, which are very important although they may *not* be close to you. These are the power factors in your life—the factors which may protect and shelter you on the one hand or may hassle and hunt you down on the other. Since we all need protection at times and are upset by hassling, it is important how we see and relate to these power factors. In this chapter we shall explore these factors and also your relationship to them.

WHAT IS AUTHORITY?

Authority is power—the power to control the behavior of people. Sometimes these people are members of an organization, a group, or a family; sometimes they are citizens of a city, state, or nation. This power may be vested in the hands of one, or in the hands of a few people. It may reside in a political party; or it may be the property of one class or ethnic group. In any event, those in authority make decisions, and those decisions are very often seen as "No's" by those who are not in authority.

One of the most pervasive and pressing problems of the present era is the problem of authority and how we react to it. Commonly expressed, it is the problem of Law and Order *versus* Freedom and Justice. Many people say we cannot have both—and if we must choose, Law and Order must necessarily come first. Others would say that without Freedom and Justice there is nothing—no humanity is left. And what point is there in having Order if this order kills the basic humanness of those who are so ordered?

Examples of this situation are found in almost every issue of our newspapers and magazines today. On the one hand protesting students on college and university campuses are said to be unruly and disrespectful. They do not obey the laws of the land—or of the campus. They do not respect the authority of the college administrators or of law enforcement agents. They do not accept the traditional values of respect for property, conformity in dress, and the need to suffer now so as to achieve status later.

On the other hand, students feel that the traditional values deny them freedom–in dress, in action, and in assembly. And they also feel that to subjugate any person or group *now* for the promise of a better future is not just—particularly when that future is one they feel they may never live to see. They see large property owners as the agents of subjugation—as agents of a kind of traditional injustice. They feel it is their right and their destiny to correct this kind of injustice.

Other examples of this kind of situation can be found in the ghettos, on Indian reservations, and even in the armed forces. Lately, groups representing the rights of women and of homosexuals have joined in the protest against presently established authority. In the words of Bob Dylan, "the times they are a-changing"; and many a father or mother, who has responsibility for Law and Order in the outside world, has found his troubles come home to roost in the behavior and attitudes of his own children.

Whatever the answer to this dilemma is, it is very clear that most of us usually resent the operation of authority when it is not in our hands, and particularly when it is exercised to control our own behavior. We resent a traffic ticket—unless it is for a person who has just endangered our safety. We are irked by tax laws and regulations—unless we are the tax assessor or collector. We object to the draft—unless we are on the draft board, or are in command of a unit of the armed services which needs manpower, or have already served and want to see that everyone else does, too. We argue against curfews—unless we are the parent or one of the adults who has set them. We riot against anti-riot laws—unless the riot is about to destroy us or our property. We strike against college or university regulations—unless we are on the Board of Trustees or are an administrative agent of the Board.

"But," you may say, "I am for traffic tickets—even when I get them. And I also am inclined to agree with the various regulations, laws, and rules mentioned above even though I am *not* a person who *has* authority or is an agent for carrying it out. I do not seem to fit into this scheme."

Your statement is most interesting and really not as unusual as it might seem. You might check this by seeing how many in your psychology class think this way about authority. For this purpose you might use the following questionnaire:

DISCOVERING HOW YOU FEEL ABOUT AUTHORITY

Encounter with Authority Questionnaire

1. When did you recently come against authority? That is, when did some person or some agency tell you to do—or not to do—something which you would not ordinarily have done otherwise? If there are several occasions, pick the incident which is *clearest* in your mind *now.* Give the time, day, and date.
2. Where did this incident take place? Give the location and the situation; for example, going home on the freeway, traffic was very heavy, weather was foggy, pavement was wet.
3. Describe the incident in detail as specifically as you can —who said what to whom? Who did what to whom? What were the responses?
4. What were your feelings while this was happening?
5. What was the final result of this incident? What did *you* finally do?
6. How did you feel *after* the incident was over?
7. How do you feel *now,* writing about the incident?

After you have filled out this questionnaire as fully as you can, and *before* you discuss these results with the other students in your class, you will find it helpful to read through the four encounters with authority which follow. These accounts were written by beginning psychology students.

Student 11

The only thing I can recall recently was an incident which happened to me the day after my 22nd birthday. It was 6:00 p.m. on Thursday, and I just got home from work. I was hot and tired after working 9 hours and I was in no mood to be hassled by anyone including my parents.

I just got into my room and barely got my jacket off when in come my parents.

All of a sudden they start hassling my mind, telling me that a certain coat hanging in the closet was mine and I kept insisting it was my brother's and it kept bouncing back and forth like a ball. I got pissed off and they got pissed off. My dad told me to knock it off and I yelled back at him and told him to knock it off. He told me that he was fed up with me and that I could leave anytime I wanted. I finally said, "Good!"

Then I stormed in and took a shower and split with a friend of mine.

I didn't see or talk to my parents off and on for over 2 weeks.

The feeling I had was resentment in the fact that they were telling me what to do and I had to put up with this for 22 years. I do feel though that they have done quite well for me and it is their house and I know I could never repay them, but I do know I have a mind of my own and that maybe someday, not only for me, but for everyone, we might be able to understand and communicate better with the older generation.

Student 12:

About two weeks ago I went to the desert for four days with a group of friends. I met a guy named Joe that I graduated from high school with and hadn't seen for three years. We rapped for quite some time and he asked if I'd like to go to the aerial tramway the next morning. I figured I'd better ask our leader or at least tell him I was going but before I could finish the leader-guy said, "No—absolutely not—you can't go!" Man—I felt like he'd slapped me or something and I just stood there and asked, "Why?" He said that already two girls had been raped (not from our group however) and that he didn't want any girl splitting off with some dude by herself.

I felt really sad that he so gruffly refused to let me go, but knowing him, that's just the way he deals with people. I even felt bad for asking to go because I should have known he had enough hassles without me adding to them.

Student 13:

It happened this last weekend at my house. I was working on some homework in the garage; there was only my mother home at the time and she was cleaning the house. She came out sort of upset so I could tell something was wrong. She said she hung up one of my jackets and had found a couple of numbers which I had forgotten about. There was nothing to say but, "Ya, ok." so she started lecturing me on the whole thing because I got busted about a month before for possession and she was upset about that, so she told me her whole thing about how she felt and finally came down and I got a chance to say something. I had a lot of arguments and a lot of her ideas were wrong but I just told her the way I felt about it and how I felt a lot safer doing this than, say, drinking, and that I planned to continue to do it. I told her the amount I smoked it and she felt better about it and could see a lot of my points. Afterwards, I went on doing my homework and she went on cleaning house and we didn't say anything more about it. I think I felt pretty good knowing at least this time I got to tell her the truth instead of a bunch of lies I made up, and she was glad to hear the truth for once, too. That night I went over to a friend's house and I wore the same jacket. The two numbers were in the pocket so me and my friend smoked them. I really felt good and I felt good that she had put them back too.

Student 14:

On April 1 (a very appropriate date), I drove down a street with which I was unfamiliar, and since there were no other cars around and no street lights, I turned on my brights because I couldn't see very well. It wasn't a through street and I turned around. I was running late and this made me even later, and I was so upset that I forgot all about my brights. I was worrying about being late and it must have been close to four minutes before I noticed a car going toward me flash its brights, and then I turned my own lights down. About a minute later a policeman pulled me over (he had been in back of me) and gave me a ticket. I was so miserable and upset that I couldn't say much of anything. My lights were already fixed and it was my first ticket, so I felt he should only have given me a warning. He was very friendly about it, but this only made me angrier. He asked me if I went to Citrus College, etc., but I felt like the hangman was trying to comfort me just before he put the noose around my neck. When he left, I started crying. Not only was I horribly late, but I got a ticket for such a stupid reason! I just regretted the whole thing terribly and wished I had never left home. The next day I was angry and felt that it was all unfair, and I wished I'd had the presence of mind to tell the policeman just how I felt. Even now when I think about it I get angry at myself for being so careless and at the policeman, both for giving me the ticket and for his manner while doing so. I don't think anyone feels much like having a cheerful conversation while they're getting a ticket!

Having read these four encounters, what are your reactions? Some of you will sympathize—feel *with* one or more of these students. some of you may feel *with* all of them. These incidents will remind you of similar incidents you have had or have heard of. You may feel inclined to defend, or attack, the actions of the students—or of the authority figures—in the incidents. It will be helpful if you will discuss and share these feelings openly and freely without trying to arrive at any decisions or pass any judgments on anybody in the incidents—if you can.

Now after you have let these feelings have free expression, for as long as it seems necessary, look at the four incidents again. Let us see if we can analyze them and by means of this analysis contribute to our understanding of authority encounters and how we can best live through them. In order to do this, ask yourself the following questions about each of the four incidents:

1. Who is the authority figure in the incident?
2. What is the crucial point of the incident, as you see it?
3. What feelings are described *during* the incident?
4. Who is the target of these feelings?
5. What are the feelings *after* the incident?
6. Who is the target of these feelings?
7. What changes in feeling, if any, took place from the start of the incident until the student's reactions after it was over?

It might be helpful to make a chart of your analysis of the four incidents, using seven columns—one for the responses to each question above. This chart will make it easier to compare the incidents.

From your analysis, who would you say are the usual authority figures students encounter? Does your experience support this conclusion?

Do you and the other students in your class agree as to what is the crucial point of each incident? How do you feel about any areas in which you disagree?

What kinds of feelings does an encounter with authority usually produce? Are these feelings pleasant or unpleasant? Are they subject to change? Or are they constant? Towards whom or what are these feelings directed?

Now you should be ready to look at and analyze your own encounters with authority, which you described with the help of the questionnaire on page 106. If these papers were done anonymously, you *may* want to exchange yours with another student. If this is not desirable, perhaps your instructor will want to chart them as you did with the four student encounters given previously. We are usually too subjective to make an effective analysis of our own behavior directly —it is too close and we feel it too intensely to "see" it clearly. For this reason it is advisable to see our behavior through someone else's eyes first.

By whatever method, a chart should be made showing an analysis of your and your fellow students' encounters with authority. You may now ask the same questions of yourselves as were asked above on page 109. But we need some additional theory in order to carry our analysis further.

HOW DO OUR FEELINGS ABOUT AUTHORITY DEVELOP?

No one can tell you *why* you feel what you do feel, or *how* you feel, or what you *should* feel. For this reason your encounter with authority is yours. However, it may be possible that your feelings are unclear or blocked—or that you do not completely understand your responses and reactions. If this is the case, it may be helpful to you to consider several theories explaining why encounters with authority take the direction, have the results, and produce the feelings which they do produce. You may then test these theories and see how they apply to you.

Talking Past the Other Person

In encounters of all kinds, the people who meet often do not talk to each other. They talk *past* each other. They talk to, or for, someone who is not present. Or they talk to themselves. As a result, the individuals involved in the encounter are so busy talking that they do not listen very much. For example, when a parent disciplines a child, he is often talking *past* the child and to a law or custom which says the child should do so-and-so.

A parent insisting on a boy's long hair being cut, or on a girl's mini-skirt being lengthened may simply be conforming to the attitudes and pressures of a hidden group—the group of adults with whom he regularly associates, but who are not present. Actually the parent may not *really* object in his own heart, but every time he sees his son's long hair, he can hear in his imagination his neighbor, Mr. Long, saying, "Don't those long-haired kids look like bums! I bet they are all on dope!" Or when he looks at his daughter's dress he hears, "Those mini-skirted girls all have loose morals. What else can they expect—showing everything they've got!"

Or he may be hearing the words of grandparents or other relatives who, in addition to the above comments, have added something to the effect that in their day children were respectful and did as they were told. Or the parent may be wrestling with himself and has thus far squelched his desire to insist on conformity in order to avoid an objectionable encounter with his son or daughter. Furthermore, he sees some legitimacy in their requests, but he feels the need to make it clear that *he* is boss; hence he lays down the law—saying to his conscience, "Now I am finally telling him/her what to do. I hope you [my conscience] are satisfied!"

In any case, the message, supposedly directed to the child, is really directed to the absent person—neighbor or relative—or to the parent's own conscience. It is usually delivered with an accompaniment of "thunder and lightning" in order to cover over the ambivalence the parent feels. Therefore, it communicates to the child *only* displeasure and sternness; the meaning is lost in emotion, and any explanation given in return is almost completely lost. It is unusual if it is even heard at all; it is certainly not listened to.

This situation is a good example of the "channel being jammed" due to emotional overloading: fear and resentment on the part of the child, anger and anxiety on the part of the parent. The sending is garbled by crossovers between the emotional and the content "tracks." And to make matters worse, neither party is at all skilled in listening: They only hear! The situation becomes extreme in emotionally loaded situations—such as the one described above—but it is present to some extent in all encounters, even in encounters between friends in a casual conversation. In encounters with authority, this is particularly true. One reason for the feelings which *develop* in authority encounters is the distance between the two individuals and the resulting confusion of messages, both verbal and nonverbal. You may be sending me, "Slow down your car for the good of all concerned on the road!" I may receive only, "I hate your guts and I don't like people with long hair!!"

For these reasons it is important to "listen" not only to words, but also to voice inflection, to facial gesture, and to body posture. And then decide, if the messages are confused, which message do I *want* to receive? Which one can I best handle?

In encounters there are *different* persons face-to-face. Assuming that they both listened and sent their messages well, there would be the additional problem that I am me and you are you. Therefore, I have a hard time putting myself in your place, and therefore, even though I get your message, I do not know what it means to be you. Often I cannot imagine how you could possibly be saying what I clearly and accurately hear. You, of course, know this quite well. For you are you, and your message makes sense in the context of you. However, you have the same difficulty with me, and cannot see how my message could possibly make sense. Of course, it may not make sense in your framework.

An example may help to make this clearer. Suppose you are a male college student about 23 years old. You are a veteran of the Viet Nam conflict and on returning have enrolled in college. I am 18, just out of high school, and am in my first year of college, too.

You have an understandable interest in the opposite sex, and since your return, have followed this interest to the fullest. I am bashful and shy, and during my high school career have "struck out" so many times that I am turned off, if not frightened, by college girls. I am, in fact, somewhat unsure of my sexual identity as a result of these failures.

We happen to be in the same class and I am attracted to you because of your openness and because you are all that I am not, but want to be. You also respond positively to me. One day you tell me of a weekend you have planned at a beach resort. You have two girls in tow. One is yours. The other can be mine if I so desire. You show me her picture to prove the fact of her desirability. You tell me other interesting anecdotes to make me aware of her qualities.

I am terribly frightened by this situation. Here is another opportunity to strike out—to meet one of those people who will want what I can't—or think I can't—deliver. I wonder, in disbelief, how you can approach such a weekend with obvious delightful anticipation.

You, on the other hand, think I am out of my mind. You think all boys had high school careers like yours. You can't believe my tentativeness. And you are finally affronted at my terrified refusal to participate in this enterprise. We both understand *clearly* each other's words—and gestures. There is no vagueness in the messages sent or received, no problem in listening. But I can't believe you—I can't even imagine you exist. And you have never heard of the likes of me. We are blocked because our two frameworks of experience are almost entirely mutually exclusive.

In this case, there is no difference in our levels of authority, but suppose I were your teacher, boss, or father: Then our encounter would be even more difficult and our resulting feelings even more confused.

"Seeing" the Other Person as Someone Else

Many times in encounters we see the other person, in part, as someone else—someone who is not present. You may unconsciously suggest to me my father or mother. I may, therefore, respond to you as I would to them. This response is, of course, subconscious. I do not know that you suggest my father to me. I only know you are domineering, authoritarian and I react violently to this behavior—as I did in the past to my father. Or you are protective, loving, and accepting, and I react positively to this behavior as I did to my mother. In many other ways you may not be *at all* like my father (or mother). But these perceptions on my part blanket everything else—and in fact simplify my reactions to you. However, it means that I understand *you* very little.

If you are in a position of authority, you may become a parent all over again. I may respond to you *as a parent,* not as a policeman, a teacher, or a boss. Since policemen, teachers, or bosses are in many ways quite different from parents—in interests and in feelings—our encounters may become charged positively or negatively—in an unrealistic way.

Encountering Oneself in the Other Person

One of the most subtle and most difficult responses in an encounter is the encounter with oneself. This kind of response is usually one of resentment. You resent the other person because he suggests yourself. In other words, you resent the you in the other person. Again, you do not *consciously* know this. But you see in him those characteristics which you despise in yourself.

The over-talkative person, particularly, resents the person who delivers a constant monologue. The overbearing person resents the policeman who gives him "the business," far more than the mild-mannered person does. The gossiper hates other gossipers. And the silent soul finds other retiring persons dull and uninteresting.

In authoritarian encounters, this situation is considerably magnified. Ask yourself why you resent some particular agent of authority. It may be because he is a shining example—*to you*—of what you consider to be your most undesirable characteristics. And this perception of him blinds you and prevents you from ever seeing him as another person or getting his message. This means that feelings—if not actions—will inevitably build up in the encounter and will tend to block any constructive result.

Releasing Strong Feelings

Many of us in encounters develop very strong feelings toward someone involved in the encounter. Sometimes it is towards ourselves, sometimes towards another person. Our four student encounters, which we analyzed earlier, are full of both kinds of feelings. In encounters with authority these feelings tend to be more extreme.

Now what do we do with these feelings? A spokesman for traditional ethics would tell us to squelch all negative feelings—and even strong positive feelings. "Better walk away from a fight or a quarrel than be carried away," "If you can't say something nice, don't say anything," "Don't wear your heart on your sleeve." We have heard these bits of advice many times.

However, feelings are energy—psychic energy—and like all energy, they cannot be destroyed. If feelings are bottled up, they are likely to break out irrationally at some unannounced, if not awkward, moment. They are likely to be displaced toward some innocent bystander. The man whose wife quarrels with him at breakfast usually takes it out on his secretary at the office. The athlete who is hassled by the football coach may take it out on his little brother when he gets home. The girl who has a row with her boyfriend may get mad at her father—for no reason. These are a few examples to show that psychic energy—feelings—cannot be destroyed, sequelched, or eliminated in any permanent way. The only way to handle them is to express them. And they *will* be expressed one way or another.

Therefore a person who enters an authority encounter with pent-up feelings is likely to unload *right there* to the disadvantage of everybody concerned. Thus, a black man in the ghetto, who has been hassled all his life by whites, may act irrationally in an encounter with a white policeman—even when the officer's intention is the best. For this reason, a black student on a college campus may react rudely and, as some would say, disrespectfully, to a white teacher who unknowingly addresses him as "boy."

Coping with Guilt Feelings

In many encounters with authority, feelings of guilt develop. This seems to be true whether the accused individual responds passively or actively. Look back at the four student encounters on pages 106–108, and you will see that before the story is ended, there are feelings of resentment and at least suggestions of guilt in three of the four situations.

Now, again, according to traditional ethics, guilt is a *desirable* result of an encounter. It makes the guilty party repent his "sin" and supposedly conditions him to avoid the guilt-producing act in the future. However, this is by no means the whole story; were the admission of guilt the only requirement for desirable behavior, psychology would be a simple matter indeed. Guilt, however, is one of the greatest destroyers of *integrity* in relationships. It is true that a guilt-ridden relationship may be solid enough for the "top-dog"—or so it may seem to him, but no guilty person can have self-integrity. Therefore, a guilt-producing relationship cannot be an integral one.

On the surface, guilt seems to "bring things into line." But only because we forget that a person who acts out of guilt resents—consciously or unconsciously—the person towards whom the act is directed.

For example, if I act in a kind and loving way toward my

mother, if I am obedient and agreeable, and if I am attentive to her needs and wishes *because of a sense of guilt*, I most surely will resent her. I am not doing what I do for her as the result of a spontaneous desire on my part to express my feelings towards her; therefore, I am glad when the attentions are over. I feel relieved. And I get no lift or satisfaction from the carrying out of my acts of "love."

If my mother has known nothing else from me, she may superficially accept this behavior and respond with apparent gratitude. However, the lack of authenticity in my behavior will come through with all of its failure to satisfy—usually in non-verbal ways—and she will demand more and more attentions and "love." She will resent any lessening in my acts of "love," and I will resent her ever-increasing and perpetual demands. Hence the falseness and duplicity in our relationship and the destructive effects upon us both will increase. We are split in ourselves between apparent "love" and actual (though perhaps unconscious) resentment. Neither of us expresses his true feelings—either because they are unconscious or because they are unacceptable. Each of us is at war within himself. The remedy for this situation is at once simple and complex. "Express your feelings authentically," we are told—and this is certainly what is needed. However, how to express ourselves after years of being split is another matter about which more will be said later. (See the section "Exploring and Releasing Your Feelings.")

Feelings and the Body

Throughout our discussion, we have discussed many aspects of feelings, but we have left out the most important one—the fact that feelings are located in the body. Often we attempt to get at, or reduce, an objectionable situation by reviewing what occurred or by trying to find a theory to explain why we acted as we did.

For example, after a row with my boss, I may become aware that I "smarted off" to him because he represents my father to me. This may be quite correct, but I may still *feel* very bad as a result of the situation. The theory didn't help.

The reason for this is that I may be acting in an *absent-bodied* way. Just as I am often absent-minded when I forget to keep my attention on the ideas about which I am supposed to be talking or thinking, so I am absent-bodied when I do not adequately pay attention to the feelings which are resident in my body.

After my encounter with my boss, I *feel* bad. This means there is a bad feeling—an objectionable feeling—somewhere in my body. By reasoning, by remembering, by rationalizing, by drinking, by theorizing, or even by sleeping, the problem—namely the bad feeling, and also my situation with my boss—does not improve. At best it may go underground, only to surface unexpectedly at a later date. If I am to get at it, I must become *present-bodied,* or embodied. I must turn off my computer—my theorizer and rationalizer—and give my attention to this feeling in my body; I must listen to my body. If I do this, I may become aware that this feeling is a knot in my stomach, or a tightness in my head, or a stiffness in my neck. This *is* the bad feeling.

Now if I will simply go *into* this feeling—for only a short time, maybe a minute or 30 seconds—and "listen," that is, be attentive to what it tells me, I may become aware that this feeling *changes* as I concentrate on it and that it starts to interpret itself to me. As this process takes place, two things happen: The feeling improves, and the feeling has words associated with it. What was first a stomach knot or a headache becomes, after a short period of concentration, a feeling of fear, of insecurity. This fear becomes localized. It is a fear of incompetence in my job and also the accompanying resentment towards my boss for making me feel this fear.

I should now feel much better in my body, because I have become *aware* of my body and also of who I am. I am an insecure person who is afraid he can't "cut it" in his job. I can now move to be more secure: I can get another job; I can seek further training; or I can discuss my feelings *with* my boss, not *at* him.

This is an example of the theory of body-awareness and how it operates in authority encounters.

The seven theoretical samples listed above are attempts to explain why certain feelings and responses do develop in authority encounters. You *only* can be the judge as to how far they apply to you and your behavior. It will help if you will share your reactions to these items with the rest of your class.

Having discussed the material in the theory section, let us see if we can apply it in several specific exercises. When these exercises are carried out in your class, you will get the most benefit from them if you volunteer to participate actively. However, if you do not feel ready to participate at first, you will want to pay very close attention to what the other students are doing. When they are involved in the exercises, you will also want to pay attention to what you yourself are feeling as you observe them. Later on, when you are ready, you will participate actively. Let us assume, however, that you have volunteered.

Step 1

To see how well you listen and also how well you can put yourself in the place of another, you will be asked to do the following:

1. You and the other students in your class select a controversial subject for discussion. What it is doesn't matter, as long as there is a definite difference of opinion on it.
2. You and a partner volunteer to take part in the exercise. One of you is in favor of the controversial question, the other is against the question.
3. You and your partner sit in chairs facing each other and close together.
4. One of you starts the debate on the question (It makes no difference who begins). You have two minutes to state your ideas. Then your partner responds for two minutes. Each of you takes his turn until the debate gets hot or each has had three or four turns.
5. Now the umpire, who may be your instructor (or better, another student), asks each of you, "Do you understand your opponent's position? Did you hear what he said?" You and your partner will probably answer "Yes". However, if you do not understand your opponent's position or did not clearly hear what he said, you ask him to please repeat. He will do the same with you. This will be continued until you are both sure that you have heard and understood what the other person said.
6. Then switch chairs. You are now your partner and your partner is you. You not only change chairs, but you also change

names and you change your sides in the argument. You act just as though you were he, and he acts as though he were you.

7. You argue in this switched position for three or four exchanges. Then you switch back to your original positions.
8. You continue doing this until you have switched positions three or four times.

Now, you and your partner tell each other, and the class (a) what your feelings were during the debate and (b) what changes of feelings you had, if any. You will then ask the class to tell you what their observations and feelings were during your debate. Finally you may want to discuss with the class how well you and your partner *did* listen to each other and how well you were each able to take the position of the other.

Step 2

Your class is asked if anyone is "hung up" on some particular question. This may be a question of guilt, as described under the heading "Coping with Guilt Feelings" above. It may be a compulsion to do or not to do a certain act (such as overeating). It may be the inability to decide on, or choose, a certain plan of action. Or it may be any of a number of other hang-ups which seem to pervade our lives today.

When you volunteer, you are asked, "Would you like to explore your hang-up? Would you like to put yourself together? Would you like to encounter yourself?"

If you would, you place two chairs close together, facing each other. You sit in one of them and are told, "There are two persons warring in you. This is what hangs you up. One of these persons is your 'top dog'. He always hassles you. The other is your 'under dog'. He always refuses to obey, to conform. Start as your top dog and tell your under dog how you feel about the hang up."

You follow these directions. After a few minutes you switch and respond as the under dog.

You continue this process for four or five exchanges.

You and the class now tell each other your feelings, observations, and reactions. During this exchange you avoid putting anyone down or telling him what he ought to have done.

You *may* become aware of how you see yourself and your relation to inner authority (top dog) more clearly. In this way, you will be moving toward healing the split which is bothering you.

Step 3

The *double chair technique* can also be used to explore, dramatically, an unsatisfactory encounter about which you still have unresolved feelings.

Your class will be asked, "Who has had an encounter with an authority figure and still has some unresolved feelings about it? Would you like to resolve some of those feelings?"

You will then be put in one of the double chairs. You are asked to talk in the *present* tense to the authority figure in the other chair as though the incident were now happening—even though the other chair is physically unoccupied. After a few broadsides, you are asked to switch chairs and be the authority figure.

These exchanges continue as long as seems practical. This exercise should release a great deal of your unresolved energy and clarify your feelings toward yourself and the authority.

You and the class will share reactions, observations, and feelings. As before, you will avoid putdowns, shoulds and oughts.

Step 4

Role playing is another technique for releasing tensions, exploring feelings, and facing authority.

For this purpose you and the class suggest several authority encounters to be played. One of these situations is selected as a starting point. Whoever suggested this situation sets the stage, picks the actors, and casts them in the roles. You start the action and go through a series of scenes using the normal role-playing procedure.[1]

Step 5

The following exercise is helpful in developing body-awareness. You sit or stretch out in the position which is most relaxing for you. Then you attempt to turn off all organized mental activity. You are told:

1. "Relax your body as much as possible. Loosen your belt or tie if you are aware of them. Take off your shoes. Close your eyes and become as fully aware of your body as possible."
2. "Start with your head and become aware of all feelings in that area of your body. Pay attention to your eyeballs, scalp, jaws, tongue, lips, and so on."

---

[1]For a discussion of role-playing techniques see Ronald Levy, *Human Relations: A Conceptual Approach*, International Textbook Co., 1969. Chapter VIII.

3. "Proceed down into your neck, shoulders, arms, chest, stomach, pelvis, legs, knees, feet, and toes. In each case, be aware of what you feel in each region."
4. "With your eyes still closed, say aloud what images come up along with these feelings: what words, what events or scenes. If a narrative seems to develop, follow it."

This exercise may be difficult for you at first. It will be easier if you follow the sequence slowly and in an unhurried fashion. With practice, you can develop great skill in body-awareness. This kind of exercise can be used to treat problems such as the one mentioned under the heading "Feelings and the Body" above.

INTERPRETING FEELINGS ABOUT AUTHORITY

The following is a case study of a student who tells of many kinds of relationships in his life. Some of them are with authority figures; some are with other persons. Read his case carefully and be prepared to discuss the following questions:

1. How would you describe Student *S*'s relationship with authority?
2. How does he respond to the attempt by someone to dominate him?
3. What feelings does he seem to have in such a situation?
4. What important things/persons seem to be missing from his life, if any?
5. In what ways, if any, is Student *S* like you?
6. What are your overall feelings about Student *S*?

The Case of Student S

My life as far back as I can remember begins when I was 7 years old and is the first significant event that I can recall.

It was my seventh birthday and I was told that I would get a bicycle for my birthday. I received the bicycle all right and was very happy with it, but the following week when I returned to school and got my bank book back I found that the $35 I had once had there was gone. I went home and asked my parents and they told me they had used the money to buy the bicycle because they didn't have the money. I couldn't understand their reason because I was so proud that I had saved this $35 out of my allowance and I couldn't understand any other reasons.

The dominance of my father also played an important part in my psychological development. My father believed that as father his position is placed at the absolute head of the household. As kids we were to have no opinions but his until we were 21 or left home. So I left home on my 18th birthday and became self-sufficient. We do get along fairly well but I was always of a fairly independent nature and liked to express my opinions openly.

When I was 15 years old and a freshman in high school I went out for "C" football. I had borrowed a set of old football cleats from a friend. I made the team and first string but at the same time those old cleats had worn out. I went to my father, told him that I made the football team and needed a new pair of football shoes. He flatly refused because he thought I should go to work and he thought athletics would ruin me. As a result I was really crushed! I had had my first chance to become a somebody and had missed the boat, but not by my doing. This is probably the most disappointing experience in my life up to now. I eventually lettered in "A" sports but I could have done much better had I been able to start earlier and with some support from my family.

One of the longest running conflicts came when I was 16 until I was 17½. I wanted to drive the car. I wanted to go out and date and all of the things centered on a driver's license. My father felt that I should wait until I was 18 but being one year younger (due to skipping 5th grade) that would put me as a freshman in college before I got my license. Everybody I knew had a driver's license; some had their own cars already and they were going to dances and doing things I wanted to do. I finally got my license, a month before graduation, and as far as high school social life, I was lacking. Some of those things I missed out on, I'm now doing with my girlfriend who is a high school senior. This way I hope to regain some of the things I lost or missed in high school.

The period of time between 16½ to 18½ years was the lowest of my life. Particularly the last year when I dropped out of school twice. The problems were all centered around girls. I had been dating different girls from time to time and there had been two who I had taken to heart. The first one played me for a fool. We had been going steady for one month and I found out that she had a boyfriend in the service who she was *engaged* to marry. I had placed a lot of trust in her and finding out about this sort of crushed me. I felt bad but the things were to get worse. Another girl came along and I was ready to be soothed and coddled by this girl and I fell again. Not because I really loved her but because she eased things for me. But she finally met a guy who really hit it off and I was flat again.

I decided to go back to work at a Boy Scout camp in the San Bernardino Mountains where I had worked for the three previous summers—just to get away from the area in which I was living.

One weekend, on my day off, I went up to a lodge near camp to see what was going on. I met a girl who worked there, and feeling lonely asked her if she wanted to go down canyon for a pizza. We went and returned, and I walked her to her door that night and decided to kiss her goodnight. Not just for the kiss but because somehow, in the short period of time I had found a personality who was connected with mine.

Now life has begun to look brighter and I'm engaged to be married. The past is dead, the future alive and happiness—I'm finding.

You have now explored relationships to authority—by means of written incidents, discussions, exercises, and by analyzing a case study. You have also read seven theoretical statements which attempt to explain how authority encounters occur and develop, and the reasons for some of the feelings which develop along with them.

It might be helpful if you would say which, if any, of these theories explains how *you* respond to authority. It might also help to ask yourself now:

Do you feel good when you meet authority?
Do you feel good *after* the encounter?
What, if anything, could you do to improve this situation?

It is your encounter. It is your response. It is your feeling. Only you can improve the situation. Finally . . .

Are you now aware of any things about yourself of which you were not aware before? Do you feel any differently about the forces of authority which you meet in your life? It might help you to do this if you would refer to the four students in Chapter 1 and see what feelings about authority they express.

HEAD PIG SAYS FIGHT
"MAN is NOT A town where
things live, but a worr
and a weeping of
an invasion of Cambodia"
WE
se of enabling Cambodia to defend its
TAKE THIS ACTION
WAR INTO
BUT

RELATIONSHIPS TO SOCIETY

6

INTRODUCTION

In the last chapter you started to investigate the authority factors in your life. You analyzed them in many ways and from many points of view. However, you never got to the point of seeing where these factors—these powers—came from.

In this chapter you will turn your attention to the gigantic organism to which both you and the power of authority belong, and as you discuss it, you may see how you and the various authorities of the last chapter are related to it.

WHAT IS SOCIETY?

Society is the mass of human individuals with whom we live. Society is not the same as family or community, for in these two kinds of associations the members have interests in common or share a common biological origin. Society is a much less personal but, in some ways, a much more definite association; in addition, society is far harder to escape from than even family.

In the past our society was limited to the individuals in a particular community—city, town, or neighborhood. Later our society meant those with whom we live in one state or nation. Today it is difficult to exclude anyone living on the earth in our definition of society.

Because it is so massive, society is quite impersonal, but it is also strong. Of course, some societies in the past have seemed weak because they crumbled and fell or decayed; however, this phenomenon may have occurred because they were *too* strong, in a rather rigid and confining way.

This strength or power is particularly noticeable when one considers the influence which society has on the person. We are born into society and, try as we may, we live and die within society. Even if we escape to the desert or the hills, we are influenced by society. It is society *from* which we are running and which determines our "escape." Your family, your schooling, your marriage, your job, your religion, even your death, are all influenced, if not determined, positively or negatively, by society, as are the laws of your community, the food which you eat, and the way you spend your free time.

Society is, then, an ever present social atmosphere, but unlike the air we breathe, society has a set of very intricate interlocking structures which sustain it—one might almost say that these structures *are* the society.

What are these structures? They are called *institutions*, but they are not the kind of institutions we mean when we refer to a college as an educational institution. The college is just one unit of the whole network of interlocking societal agencies which we refer to as "the institution of education." We cannot possible "see" or even completely understand or appreciate the whole of the institution of education in our society; however, like a huge girder under a bridge, it supports us. If we think about it, we know that it must be there. We glimpse parts of it when we look at the bridge from a distance. The same is true of the other institutions which make up society. Perhaps it would help to describe a few of the more important institutions which make up society; doing so may help us to see a bit more clearly what society is and how we react and relate to it.

The Family

The family is perhaps the oldest and best known institution of society. Most of us who were not orphans or abandoned were born *into* a family. And our family is one example of the institution which we call "The Family." Most families today were sanctioned by some religious organization; the family structure of one husband and one wife is also legally sanctioned. A husband and wife make certain pledges to each other publicly, and some, if not all, of these pledges may be enforced by the laws of the land. Such families are almost always located in one house or apartment and live there more or less permanently. The family, however, does not have this structure in all cultures and at all times. In the culture of the slums of Mexico City, Oscar Lewis[1] tells us that few, if any, families are blessed by any formal ceremony or sanctioned by any sort of legal license. However the "husbands" seem to have a great sense of responsibility and a considerable degree of fidelity, even though they may support and look after several "wives," each of whom lives with her children in separate living quarters.

---

[1] Oscar Lewis, *The Children of Sanchez* (New York: Vintage Books, 1961).

In the days of the Old Testament patriarchs, families were nomadic, following the grazing of their cattle, sheep, and goats. They had no fixed location at all. There was one father or husband, but he usually had many wives and also many concubines. Those concubines were women living with the family by whom the husband could have children, but who had fewer legal rights than the wives. In no case was the husband married or bound to the concubines by either religious or legal bonds.

In many of the island cultures of the South Pacific, families are matriarchal in nature. The mother, or wife, is the adviser and leader of the family, and often there are many husbands who live with her and her children.

In still other cultures, men and women may live together communally, each one cohabiting and having sexual intercourse according to his choice. Children from these unions are the responsibility of all the adults of the commune. In these communal "families" there is rarely any ceremony sanctioning the choice of living together and only the law of mutual responsibility to hold the group together and to provide for the children.

From these few examples it is obvious that the institution which we call The Family is subject to much variation in its specific examples. In most, if not all, societies, however, there are families to which most individuals belong. The big question is: How does anyone *feel* about his family? How do you feel about *your* family? Is it your own specific family which turns you off—or on? Or is the whole idea of a family objectionable? or a great source of security and pleasure to you?

Education

If the family is the oldest institution of society, education must have come soon afterwards, for the young of any family can only be brought up at home for a limited number of years. It is true that they may learn at home how to adjust to the rigors of living with adults; they may, and do, watch and learn from what mother does in and around the house (or cave, in more ancient times). And they can also learn, by watching father, how to be head of the family, or boss, how to get along with the opposite sex, and how to "bring home the bacon." But during a period beginning at somewhere between six and ten years of age, children—particularly boys—must be sent out of the home to learn about the outside world and about how to navigate the passage between childhood and adulthood over the difficult sea of adolescence.

For this "out of the home" education, schools, colleges, and universities are instituted, and it is these facilities which make up what is usually called the Educational Institution of society. But just as separate families are only loosely organized into what we call the Family in most societies, so schools, colleges, and universities are only loosely organized in the Educational Institution—at least in the United States at present.

Each state of the United States has a somewhat loosely organized system of public elementary schools and high schools and a separate system of tax-supported colleges and universities. Private schools, at all levels, exist for the most part outside of this system. There is virtually no overall organization of the various school systems of the fifty states.

In foreign countries the pattern varies. Many countries do have some form of a national education system, but it by no means includes all educational institutions. Furthermore, there are the various systems of religious or parochial schools and colleges, both in America and elsewhere. These religious schools are almost entirely separate from other non-religious private schools as well as from the tax-supported public schools.

In the past the Educational Institution was even more loosely organized than it is today. A few city-states, such as Sparta, had a rigorous system of education for boys of a particular social class. But generally, as families joined to become clans, and clans formed into villages, villages grew to become towns, towns became cities, and cities developed their own national identities, schools became more numerous and usually less organized as far as any overall pattern was concerned.

Systems of education developed usually only when one school seemed in danger of educating for some value which was considered by the governing powers to be against the national, state, or community interests, or when a school was neglecting to educate for a value which was considered essential by the governing powers. For example, in Massachusetts in the 1840's, it was considered undesirable to teach any form of religion in the public schools, since no church or religious group in the community wanted any other church or religious group to be in control of this phase of education. Therefore, all religious education in public schools was ruled out by the governing boards, and this practice has generally been followed until the present. For many years we have considered patriotism and loyalty essential values to teach in the schools. These values were taken for granted in most parts of the United States until after World War II. Since then, a great fear of Communism has developed in the United States. Therefore, American flags are displayed in all classrooms, pledges of allegiance are almost universally administered, and loyalty oaths are required of most school and college personnel. These practices were required by governing boards in their attempt to be sure that schools developed the value of loyalty in their students. These boards gave little consideration to how effective these practices were. Nevertheless, it is the necessity for instituting controls which moves the separate educational institutions into a more unified educational system. If the lessons of Nazi Germany are to be considered, one would suspect that there is a limit beyond which system control would be damaging to the learning processes which are supposed to go on in schools and colleges. We should, then, quite properly ask, Is our Educational Institution too rigidly unified? You might ask yourself, How do I feel about my past experience in schools? How do I feel about my present college experience? Do I feel that my educational experience was too regimented? Or was it too loosely controlled? Has this experience in school and college been a good trip? Or was it a bad one? What seemed to make it that way?

Religion

Along with the Family and Education, Religion is an early and very important institution of society. The family gave early man a kind of warmth and security. Education trained the young of the family to get along in society. But religion answered—or tried to answer—questions about the non-material side of his existence. Early in his life, man was frightened by the powers of nature—by the wind, by storms, by fire, by lightning, by thunder, by earthquakes. He was also perplexed, if not frightened, by death, and by birth, by seasonal changes from month to month, by daily changes from hour to hour, by light and dark, not to mention celestial objects and phenomena, and also by the processes of growth and decay. He could control few, if any, of these aspects of his existence, but their influence was powerful. He therefore searched for some way to understand them, to anticipate them, and to live with them in a certain degree of harmony. Those of the family, tribe, or clan who were most skilled in dealing with abstract ideas became leaders in this activity. Perhaps they may have been those less skilled in other more physical activities, such as hunting. Eventually the role of these seekers–or seers–became institutionalized. They were set apart to perform a separate function for the society. It seemed that they could get better insights, revelations, and visions when separated from the normal interference of everyday activities. The seers—medicine men, shamans, priests, and the like, were therefore housed in a separate building, or place, usually called a temple (in Latin this was the *fanum*). That which went on inside the temple was related to the power, or powers, which controlled all of the mysteries and events which frightened or perplexed man. This power was called God, and the activities which pertained to God—ceremonies, sacrifices, or rites—were called sacred. The temple was therefore the place for that which was sacred, and it was watched over and controlled by those who were sacred, the priests. That which took place outside of the temple was profane. Those people or events who were outside were therefore profane. It was important to keep what belonged in the temple safely in the temple and to keep what belonged outside the temple outside. It was a great sin to mix language, people, or events which belonged in one place with those which belonged in the other. If this were done, the effectiveness of the temple and the priests would be reduced, if not destroyed, and the search for more effective relationships with the All Powerful would be blocked. Hence sacred and profane were separate categories in the religious institutions of society.

Today this situation has hardly changed. Whatever kind of religious institution you attend or are affiliated with—whether it is a temple, a synagogue, a church, a meeting house, or a mosque–that which goes on *inside* is sacred and must not be mixed with the profane outside world—except when the outsiders enter with a sacred attitude and in a sacred manner. The affairs of man are profane and belong outside. The affairs of God are sacred and belong inside.

But what happens when a social upheaval, or revolution, convulses the sacred and profane in one society-shattering explosion—such as in the Russian revolution, or in the Reformation, or in the Holy Land at the time of the Crusades, or in the Spanish Civil War, or in Israel today? What happens when the youth of the day become upset and disillusioned with the sacred activities of the "temple" and feel these ceremonies give little insight into their problems or help in developing an effective life style? At such times, if and when they occur, the sacred may be forcefully profaned; that is, it may be attacked and controlled by elements of the profane outside world. Or the sacred may find itself painfully close to being isolated, while society deserts it and its ceremonies for a more direct attack on the problems which are all too pressing and crucial in the outside world. At such times the airtight division between the sacred and the profane comes into question. And many observers believe that the present is such a time.

Now, how do you feel about the religious institution with which you identify yourself—church, temple, or whatever? How do you feel about religious institutions in general? What necessary function (if any) do these institutions serve today? Has man fully explained his relationship to that which is greater than himself—perhaps by means of science? Or are there still unknowns and unknowables, imponderables which will always call on the special skills, special personalities, and special ceremonies of a kind of sacredness to which we should all give reverence? Only you can answer these questions for yourself. Or do you feel that they are not even worth answering?

Business and Industry

The need for some form of manufacturing came much later in the history of man's development than the need for family, education, or religion. It was not until man made goods for, or rendered services to, a much wider community than his family, that the need for some form of business and industry developed.

Prior to this time a man might have some excess food or an extra tool or weapon which he would keep in a safe place. His skills at hunting, building, healing, protecting, or decorating would be largely for his own family's use—or at most for the benefit of his clan. As his skills became more creative and productive, however, he might especially enjoy making one particular product—drums, for example; or performing one particular service—healing, for instance. Neighbors, other clan or tribe members, or even men from great distances might come to get his drums, or have their fevers and madnesses healed by him. His reputation might then spread far and wide as a great drum-maker, or a great medicine man. In such cases there would need to be some way to "pay for" these goods and services.

At first the "pay" would be other goods. The drum-maker would set the "price" of his drum at so many reindeer pelts. Or the medicine man might set the price of his healing a bad fever at so many humming-bird wings. This, of course, is the barter system.

Later on some particular goods—say sea shells of a particular kind—would be the medium of exchange. Still later on it might be pieces of metal, gold dust, or precious stones. Finally metal coins of particular sizes were made, followed by paper money, personal checks, and finally, that financial marvel of all marvels, the credit card.

Thus, it is clear that as goods and services are produced in a more specialized and more widely distributed way a need arises for some medium of exchange. Along with this a need arises to account for what is sold, to anticipate what will be sold, to distribute or store the goods which have been manufactured, and to advertise what goods and services are available.

These complex needs would quickly get in each other's way if they were not organized. Even the neighborhood tailor, shoemaker, or cleaner must be concerned with the two sides of his operation: the production or giving of services, and the organization and distribution of the goods and services produced. These two phases *roughly* correspond to what we mean today by business and industry. Although business and industry are usually concerned with *both* of these phases, business usually stresses the organization and distribution of goods and services, whereas industry is concerned with manufacture primarily.

Today, however, we have fewer and fewer neighborhood businesses, stores, craftsmen, and markets. They are very rapidly being swallowed up by large enterprises which form huge networks of stores, markets, cleaning and repair services, and utilities. In most of these enterprises production and distribution and organization and advertising are all part of one interlocking whole. Business and industry are so clearly intermeshed that they are impossible to separate. Furthermore the large corporations invest in each other's stocks and also the same individuals may be on the board of directors of many corporations. This whole gigantic complex has spanned the oceans and is world-wide. It is for this reason that we often refer to it as the business and industrial complex. And it is this complex which is called the Institution of Business and Industry. It is probably the most tightly organized, enormous, and powerful of all the institutions of society.

Now that we know to some degree what makes up the complex institution of Business and Industry, let us ask some questions about it.

Of course, the first question is, What are your feelings about this institution? Does it give you a sense of security? A sense of fear? Or a sense of being trapped or controlled by it? Would you like to be a part of such an enterprise? If so, what kind of business or industry? Do you feel that Business and Industry has any role in society other than making profit and producing goods? If so what is this role? Do you have particular feelings towards certain businesses or industries? If so, what are they? What rewards do you feel someone could expect to get from working in a business or industry?

Government

The need for some form of government arises at almost the same time in the history of man's development as the need for a rudimentary system of business and industry. For just as the endeavor of providing goods and services requires some kind of organization and control, so do all the affairs and activities of men need organization and control—or so we are told.

In the beginning, the father was the "boss" of the family—at least in the patriarchial system. He said who was to do what and when he was to do it. If there were any rules, he made them. In time of stress and danger, he was the protector and provider. If there were arguments, he settled them, and he also punished all wrong-doers. There was one such "boss" for each family.

As a family or clan grew, one particular person became responsible for ruling the whole clan. He (or she) was usually a person of seniority who was also outstanding in respect to some particular characteristic: strength, wisdom, or endurance, for example. He ruled all the affairs within the families of his clan.

Societal units continued to grow and became more complex. Clans united to become tribes. Tribes settled down in one spot and nations emerged. Today we have various organizations of nations, but all of them seem to be relatively weak compared to the strength of the individual nations which compose them. Those people who expect strong government above the national level are probably dealing more with wishes than with reality.

But how can the affairs of men be organized within and between these societal units? Originally the pattern of the patriarchy was simply expanded. If father could run the family, and a "senior father" could rule a clan, why couldn't an earl, a duke, a prince, or a king rule his state or nation? Thus the feudal system was born.

The feudal lord, king, duke, or other leader was the head of the estate. He lived in his castle and he and his henchmen controlled, patrolled, taxed, and defended all the vassals in his fief. They all owed him allegiance in case of war or invasion, and he owed them protection. He was judge and jury for all disputes. In many cases he was the executioner as well. He could, and often did, call on the local official of the church in his area—usually a bishop or archbishop—to help settle a dispute or to reinforce his judgment. This strategy was quite effective since at the time nearly everyone was a member of the Church. There was only one church—at least in Europe. Written laws were few. Those laws which were written were usually church laws. Most people, whether lords or vassals, were illiterate. In most cases the feudal lord *was* the law.

As ocean navigation became more dependable, foreign trade—particularly with the Orient—developed, and the mercantile system grew. Along with this development came a need to produce more goods at home, and so business and industry became a necessary aspect of society. This development meant that the power of a nation or state was no longer in the hands of the feudal lord, who inherited his throne, nor in the hands of the princes of the church, who achieved their power by study, commitment, and ordination. Power now belonged to the merchant "princes" and to the "captains" of industry, who controlled the economic instruments and the capital of the nation. "He who controls the credit makes the decisions" became the watchword. Capitalism burst into full flower, and feudalism gradually died. With this change in economic structure, there followed a governmental change, for now inherited and ordained power was no longer acceptable, the people demanded, and got, the right to rule, or select rulers, and middle-class, representative democracy was born.

Since then, the continuing debate and struggle has been over the question of who should select the rulers and decision-makers of a nation? At first only property-owning merchants and landlords were allowed to participate. "Life, liberty, and property" was almost written into the Declaration of Independence of the Thirteen Colonies from the British Crown. Later on, all races of men—in theory at least—were given the right to be represented and to vote. Congress was also prevented from making any law "respecting an established religion." And finally—much later—women were admitted into the community of voters, representatives, and decision-makers.

During this period of change in governmental structure, the population of the nations of the world increased enormously. Therefore, the governmental structure, which was esentially designed for relatively small, and at best, newly emerged industrial nations, became badly suited to the governing of large and powerfully growing economic enterprises. One had to ask frequently, "Who is controlling the affairs of government? Is it the voters and their representatives? Or is it the leaders of business and industry?" There were attempts to change the governmental structure, but these changes often came about too slowly or with great difficulty. An illustration of this lag is the length of time between the U.S. Supreme Court's decision on school desegregation in 1954 and its only piecemeal implementation at present, by which time some people are saying that desegregation is no longer what is needed.

These are all very controversial questions. If you poll your friends, you are quite likely to find a wide range of opinions and attitudes regarding the questions raised in the preceding paragraph. An equally wide spread of opinions exists among politicians and "experts" in political science. On one item, however, there is little if any controversy: everyone agrees that government is now one of the most powerful institutions of society and seems destined to become even more powerful.

How, then, do you *feel* about all this? You have read the brief history above of the development of our governmental system. Does it agree with your experience and knowledge? If not, in which way is the description in error? What do you feel about the present state of our governmental system—at the national, state, and municipal levels? Is there any hope, or any need, for an international government? As one of the most powerful institutions of society, what does our system of government do for you? Does it turn you on or off? Do you identify with it at all? Or would you prefer to ignore it and eliminate governmental concerns from your life entirely?

The Military

The Military is really an aspect of government, or a branch of government. However, today, in a world pervaded by war—both actual and potential—the power, numbers, and influence of the Military is growing very rapidly. By "The Military" we mean all of those aspects of our society which are concerned with war—either attempting to avoid or prevent it, or engaged in carrying it on.

Originally each man was his own military department. He protected himself, and his family, with whatever weapons he could make: clubs, bows and arrows, spears, and so on. He might also invade other families or clans to obtain food or women, or to satisfy other needs. He, along with his fellow tribesmen, might contest with another tribe over the right to hunt or fish in a certain area. Usually these military efforts grew out of scarcity of or dire need for some particular life necessity. When times were good and the supply was plentiful, the affairs of men would be peaceful.

As communities grew and governments became more complex, the distribution of goods was not so easily accomplished. Furthermore, the dependence of an agricultural society on the weather and other forces of nature could often cause famine and scarcity. A peaceful migrant tribe might become militant marauders in the face of starvation. Once people have learned the ways of war, they may find it hard to settle down and depend on nature, or on the benevolence of fellow man, with any great amount of security. Therefore, it may often be easier to convert plowshares into spears than to accomplish the reverse. This problem is not so much a matter of difficulty with the metal as a matter of difficulty with the psyches of those who have once been committed to war.

For whatever reasons, military activities and governments grew almost as twins. In ancient Greece the ideal governments described by Plato and Aristotle needed the Military not only as a means of defense, but also in order to acquire slaves and occasionally to increase territory. In many ways these same three reasons are used to justify the need for the Military today–although the term "slave" is repugnant to us.

With the discovery of gunpowder and later of nitroglycerine, TNT, and atomic and hydrogen bombs—not to mention gases, and other chemical agents of destruction—the waging of war and the organization of the Military have become increasingly complex and expensive. War was easily extended to ships on the seas, and now we use not only jet aircraft, but also rockets of every description and power which race through the air. These agents of rapid and accurate transportation have further complicated our military system and made it possible for us mutually to destroy ourselves and our enemies in a matter of minutes. In a sense, we hover at the brink of Armageddon and are held back from it only by the fear of the result. Yet those persons in control cannot seem to loose their hold of these instruments, or even to reduce their accumulated destructive power, because of what *they*—the other side—might do. Leaders of nations seem to feel that an accumulation of "over-kill" will prevent the enemy from using his destructive power on them —and the enemy evidently thinks the same thing. Hence the military activity is much less one of actual conquest of land, than it is conquest for bases, for air space, for new explosives, and for transportation agents. All of these activities have made the Military one of the most expensive activities of modern society. Its budget is secondary to very few, if any, of our other governmental agencies.

Its manpower grows. And along with these developments are the increased power and influence which the Military exerts upon Business and Industry, the institution which must produce the materials and instruments for war; upon Education, the institution which must train the skilled manpower; on the Family, the institution which must produce the manpower; and on Government, the institution which must through its various agencies supply the money and also absorb the huge military machine into its own organization without being swallowed by it in the process. Interpreting and understanding the Military as an institution of our society thus becomes a real problem. In the past the Military was simply one small agency of government, but today no description of society which did not give to the Military a very prominent part, at least, equal to that of any other institution of society, could possibly be realistic.

For some of us this state of affairs may appear to be very tragic. We do not like to think of ourselves as a warlike or war-making nation—regardless of which nation we live in—and the developments described above are applicable more and more to *all* the nations of the world. Others of us feel that this state of affairs is as it should be. We are aware of the expense and increased power, but we see the situation as little different from many of the eras in the past—pre-Christian Rome, for example—when military activities were a way of life.

As a student of psychology, how do you feel about the Military? First, do you feel that the description of the state of affairs in the preceding paragraphs is accurate? It not, how would you modify this description? Some of you may have served in the Military, either in Viet Nam or elsewhere. What is your feeling about the Military? Others of you—women, for example—are not personally involved with military service. How do you feel about it? Do you feel this institution of our society is at all out of balance with respect to others? Do you feel its place and emphasis are quite in order? Do you see the Military as an object of pride? Of fear? Of security? Or is it too complicated to be concerned and involved with at all? In any case your feelings about it are *yours* and as such are very important.

You have now read about six of the important institutions of society. They certainly are not all of the societal institutions; however, they probably do have more influence on most of us than any of the others. You are now ready to see how you can apply this theoretical knowledge.

DISCOVERING HOW YOU FEEL ABOUT PARTICULAR INSTITUTIONS

Now that you have read about society and discussed some of your feelings and reactions to it, it is time to get more fully into your personal reactions. For this purpose the following questionnaire has been prepared.

Feelings And Reactions to Society Questionnaire

1. You have read about six of the important institutions of society. In these institutions there are many groups of people who together help those institutions to function. Listed below are several of these groups. Look at the list carefully, and circle those which seem to be important to you.

Family members	Workers
Consumers	Politicians
Students	Law Enforcement
Religious groups	Managers
Members of the Military	Citizens
Teachers	Agents

2. Are there other institutional groups (not friends or social companions) which you feel are important to you which are not mentioned above? If so, what are they?
3. To which of the groups mentioned in questions 1 and 2 do you belong?
4. Towards which of the groups in questions 1 and 2 do you feel positive? Which ones do you like?
5. Towards which of these groups do you feel negative? Which ones do you reject?
6. In a complex society, such as the one we all live in, there are many problems to be worked out. Each of us has his own style of working them out. What do you feel is the best way—the way *you* would choose—to work out the problems of living in today's society?
7. How, if at all, do you feel that the established society of today should be changed?

8. In a short paragraph, describe today's society, telling how you see it, how you feel about it, and how it operates as far as you are concerned.

After you have filled out this questionnaire, it will be important to compare your answers with those of the other students in your class. If you fill out your questionnaire anonymously, you can probably be more free in sharing, discussing, and tabulating the results.

DISCOVERING AND INTERPRETING YOUR FEELINGS ABOUT SOCIETY

The following are the reactions of several psychology students to items 6, 7, and 8 of the *Feeling and Reactions to Society Questionnaire.* Read them carefully and consider them in the light of the questions which follow on page 144. You will notice that the questions are included only for student 15.

Student 15

6. In a complex society, such as the one we all live in, there are many problems to be worked out. Each of us has his own style of working them out. What do you feel is the best way—the way you would choose—to work out the problems of living in today's society?

To try and cope with the problems and live a life that fits you the best.

7. How, if at all, do you feel that the established society of today should be changed?

Trying to stop violence, by peace and harmony, and eliminating corruption.

8. In a short paragraph, describe today's society, telling how you see it, how you feel about it, and how it operates as far as you are concerned.

Today's society is a lot more aware of its problems and tries to change (sometimes for the good and other times not) them. I think there are a lot of people who are against society as it is, and want a change. If people can get together on these different problems and try to solve them logically, it might help. I feel some change in society will come up soon. What exactly it is, I'm not sure.

Student 16

6. Swing with the establishment.

7. Do away with racism, have a minimum income for those who need it, have free or reasonably priced medical care for everyone, spread the wealth, shift to socialism, shift from a militarily run government, get rid of military-industrial complex.

8. The U.S. is a racist society, run by the military-industrial complex, with a war-oriented economy. A rich country where some people are starving. I feel pretty badly about it and think we need a change.

Student 17

6. It's hard for me but I feel faith and trust can help us. For everyone to come together instead of standing at four corners. Even and balanced discussion. I feel anything is worth at least a try.

7. I feel that everything in our nation's power should be done to stop riots and help these people see that they're harming us more than helping to change. How we'll do this I don't know!

8. Today is better and more comfortable than we've ever known it. Modern conveniences and facilities, great recreation areas. But what about the starving—while we're enjoying people are starving. There should be more help now toward fellow man—more forgiveness and certainly more understanding.

Student 18

6. Strive to understand yourself and your feelings so that you may be able to better know why others do whatever they do.

7. Well, I don't know if this pertains to the subject but it does to me! Society should regulate the prices of food and other items so people will treat each other like people instead of running over each other.

8. Today, society *in America* is a rat race with people running over other people just to get their almighty dollar. Not enough people are willing to just talk with each other and take it easy. Everything is hurry, hurry, hurry and in the end, all we are doing is hurrying to our graves.

Student 19

6. Be yourself, stand on steady ground, show love and kindness, be honest, most of all be at peace with yourself and with God.
7. Accept people for what they are; judge their character not their color, creed, or ideology.
8. Chaotic group of people grasping out for something and I'm afraid going in all wrong direction, backwards. We must stop or we will all kill each other, by no one's choice. Survival of the fittest—the wrong way, the road to Death.

Student 20

6. "React as the masses react!"
7. "Do what you feel is important and can or will benefit someone other than just yourself!"
8. "Our society is crumbling around us, because of a lack of communication between our government and us (public)—parent & child—*one human being to another.* Sometime during the last 10 years, our government has *lost* its *greatest* and most *important* asset which is *its former ability to communicate with its people, the needs and desires of the country . . . and to instill in the people the willingness to do their duty as an American citizen!" Vote etc.*

Student 21

6. Look at it, accept what you see, understand what you see.
7. Society today should eliminate the goals based on money and power.
8. I see our society as a power seeking and money hungry animal that is out of touch with the realities that govern and control the universe. I see money as the evil which rots out the hearts of men and turns them cold. I also see a new age coming upon man where peace and brotherhood are the goals to strive for—not money. I feel good—damn good—to know that in a society which predominates with evil, there are people who seek to spread peace and brotherhood. Peace.

Student 22

6. A person needs to cope with the surroundings and their fellow men. They need to know and understand the why and how of things and then to find answers to these why's and how's.
7. It's being changed slowly but surely!

8. Today's society is going through a trying period or you could say through a big change. The younger generation is experiencing this change because they are a part of it. I feel this way because it's happening—you can see it all over. There may be riots and fires and demonstrations but these are causing higher officials to look farther than the end of their desks.

Questions about
the student responses
to the "Feelings and Reactions
to Society Questionnaire"

1. Do you see any agreement among the responses to question 6? Do any of these responses agree with the predominant responses in your class? With yours?
2. In the responses to question 7, are the suggested changes realistic? Do they give a hint as to the student's attitudes towards society? How do these agree with you? With your class?
3. In question 8, students went to great length to express their ideas, but they revealed attitudes, too. What attitudes do you find revealed in these responses? Can you see how these attitudes may be related to attitudes toward authority or self as discussed in the previous chapters?
4. Are there any consistencies in the picture of society given by these students in their responses to 8?
5. Are the responses to 8 consistent with the responses to 6 and 7 for each student? Can you suggest what attitudes and feelings may be behind any inconsistencies in the responses to these three items?
6. Now analyze your own responses to 8 in a similar way.

We have covered your relationship to society as a whole through various exercises in the last part of this chapter. As a concluding exercise, let us look back to the questions at the end of each of the six sub-sections of the section headed "What is Society?". Now answer these questions and list your answers together on one sheet of paper. As you look at these answers, what feelings and reactions do you have? Are there any additional things you now want to say about society? If so, write them in a few sentences and compare them with what you already wrote in answering the questions about the student responses. This exercise may give you some new insights.

RELATIONSHIPS TO SOCIETY

Finally, how do you think the four students in Chapter 1 feel about society? How might they answer questions 6, 7, and 8 of the *Feelings and Reactions to Society Questionnaire?* Which one of them would have answers most like yours?

"MAN is NOT A town wher
things live, but a worr
and a weeping of w wings
invasion of Cambodia"
of enabling Cambodia to defend its
AKE THIS ACTION

7

CONCLUSION: WHERE IS YOUR HEAD AT NOW?

CONCLUSION: WHERE IS YOUR HEAD AT NOW?

At the beginning of this book, you started on a trip with four students: Joe, Sylvia, Randy and Janie; remember them? Then you proceeded—partly by yourself and partly with your class—to look at your relationships in various aspects of your life. You rapped about your peers. You looked at your self and your roots. You explored your reactions to authority and its hassles. You tied in all you had learned with your ideas about society and the Establishment.

Now it may look as if your job is finished. It isn't. The heaviest job is still ahead of you. It's a hard heavy and a good heavy at the same time, because *you* now have to add it up and see—after all this discussion—where you really are at.

The following pages are blank. To finish this trip and do a really complete job, you have to get into the act right here *in the book*. You may have some conclusions you want to put down. You may have some questions to ask. You may have a whole load of gripes and want to tell what a bad idea this all was. Or you may have had some really groovy experiences. Whatever it is, *you* write it—and if these pages aren't enough, I am sure your instructor can supply more. Remember that it's *your* self, *your* life, *your* peers and *your* society. So tell it the way *you* feel it!

APPENDIX

OBSERVING AND RECORDING GROUP PROCESSES

In established groups it is the practice to have a secretary who keeps minutes. This is exactly what a group observer-recorder does *not* want to be. The secretary is concerned with business minutes: little things which really don't matter to anyone, about which no one *feels* anything, and which are only done compulsively, because some set of external rules says that's the way to do it. They are done in conformity to a lot of "shoulds" and "should nots."

In contrast to this method, the observer-recorder has no set form to follow in observing and recording. He needs to be sensitive to the group, its pulse, and its atmosphere. And he can be sensitive to them only if he is sensitive to himself.

Sensitivity does not come in some predetermined package or by some set formula. It comes by turning off other concerns and relaxing both body and mind (which really are one) so as to pick up whatever is going on in and around oneself. For this reason the group needs to be as relaxed and free of tension as possible, and the observer should be particularly relaxed. His pencil need not be poised for action, but his body and his sensory equipment should be alive. In this condition his report will also tend to be alive.

But the problem is that language and compulsive language instruction may easily hang up the observer. He may observe quite well; but when he writes, he goes back to all those old fears, anxieties, and compulsions of spelling, punctuation, and grammar which can block the communication of feelings so effectively if he has been intimidated by diagrammed sentences and threatened by commas and spelling rules. Therefore, he should disregard all his compulsive language experiences and simply write as naturally as possible—as he sees and feels.

1. You are in the meeting *now*. Write in the *present* tense. Your report will be finished when the meeting is over. Don't polish it or worry about its form or smoothness. Human experiences are often rough and therefore need to be reported roughly.
2. Be personal! Say what you feel and observe what others do. Don't be general and impersonal. Mention names and specifics.
3. *As nearly as possible* don't put anyone down—even yourself. Therefore, *try* to eliminate "shoulds" and "shouldn'ts". But if they occur, they are. So are your observations. Therefore report them!
4. What is said in words is often much less important than what is said by look, facial expression, voice tone, gesture, or body posture.
5. Your personal feelings are often a clue to what is going on in the group. However, take responsibility for your feelings. Say "I feel . . ." rather than "Everyone is . . ." unless you have some evidence of how everyone feels.
6. Don't worry whether the group will agree with what you observe. These observations are yours. Do *you* agree with them? The other group members will read your report and will air or write their differences with you. This does not mean that you are wrong. It simply means that we all see things a bit differently, but not completely differently.

Now, what exactly should you look for? Of course there are many things—far more than anyone could be attentive to at once. Some of these are the pattern of participation, the roles played, the atmosphere, the camouflage and put-downs, the eye-contact. These aspects and many others have been explained often in other publications. One place to get more details on how to deal with these specifics of group operations is *Human Relations: A Conceptual Approach,* pp. 182–189. This book was already mentioned on p. 120.

INDEX